SCIENCE, TECHNOLOGY,

AND GOVERNMENT FOR

A CHANGING WORLD

APRIL 1993

THE CONCLUDING REPORT OF THE

CARNEGIE COMMISSION
ON SCIENCE, TECHNOLOGY, AND GOVERNMENT

ISBN 1-881054-11-x

Printed in the United States of America

SCIENCE, TECHNOLOGY, AND GOVERNMENT FOR A CHANGING WORLD

CONTENTS

FOREWORD

DAVID A. HAMBURG
President
Carnegie Corporation of New York

S cience is not a separate entity, remote from the lives of people. Indeed, science provides the basis for most of the requirements of modern living: the world has been transformed by science and technology in this century and this transformation is continuing, even accelerating, as the century comes to its close.

In the early 1980s, I became increasingly impressed with the profound difficulty for governments of meeting the challenge of accelerating scientific and technological developments. These concerns led me to convene a group of distinguished scientists at Carnegie Corporation of New York. They shared my concerns and strengthened my inclination to organize a Carnegie Commission on Science, Technology, and Government (CCSTG).

A vital turning point in the development of the Commission occurred when I was able to enlist the distinguished leadership of Joshua Lederberg and William Golden as co-chairs, and then to enlist President Carter as a Commission member and President Ford as an Advisory Council member. These appointments ensured that the Commission work would be of the highest quality and that it would be relevant to the emerging problems of American society. Still, I was not prepared for the enormous outpouring of interest and effort on the part of the many people who have come to form the Commission family (Appendix D), and to whom I express my deepest gratitude.

In the years since its establishment, the Commission has deepened our understanding of the important role science and technology can play in meeting the challenges of the human future—for example, in reducing the economic and social disparities between the Southern and Northern Hemispheres; in sustaining long-term economic growth while at the same time respecting the environment; and in creating and maintaining peaceful relations among nations in the post–Cold War world.

The CCSTG has produced a set of reports that are highly diverse, intellectually rich, and practical in application. The main themes are likely to be useful for decades to come. They provide variations on one basic, underlying theme: the search for judicious use of science and technology in the context of humane, democratic values. If this work is taken seriously by leaders and incorporated into the work of the relevant institutions, the world will become a much better place than it is now.

David A. Hamburg

PREAMBLE AND HIGHLIGHTS OF THE COMMISSION'S RECOMMENDATIONS

Joshua Lederberg
University Professor
Rockefeller University

Government is the complex of institutions, laws, customs, and personalities through which a political unit exercises power and serves its constituencies.

Science is the search for novel and significant truths about the natural world. These truths are usually validated by the prediction of natural phenomena and the outcome of critical experiments.

Technology is the instrumental use of scientific knowledge to provide, for example, goods and services necessary for human sustenance and comfort and to support other, sometimes contradictory aims of the political authority.

Scientific expertise and technology have always been valued by government. Weapons and medicines, maps and microprocessors: the products of science are indispensable to successful government. So, increasingly, is scientific thinking. Where but to science can society turn for objective analysis of technical affairs?

The scientific mind can bring much to the political process. But science and politics are a hard match. Truth is the imperative of science; it is not always the first goal of political affairs. Science can be, often should be, a nuisance to the established order, much as technology often bolsters it.

Moreover, many scientists, lacking the policy skills needed to relate their expertise to social action, are uncomfortable dealing with the political machinery.

A vital responsibility of the expert advisor is to clarify technical issues so that the essential policy questions become accessible to the judgment of the community at large.

Yet expertise also has distortions, arising from conflicts of interest, differing levels of competence, peculiarly posed questions, and cultural biases. The discipline of the peer group is the main source of the authenticity of the scientific community.

Science, in fact, cannot exist without a community of scientists, a forum for organized, relentless skepticism of novel claims. Science kept in confidence and inaccessible to colleagues' criticism is no longer authentic. The public rendering of advice and defense of conclusions is of the utmost importance. Nevertheless, advice within the political system must often be confidential. Herein lies another structural contradiction and challenge to the design of organization and decision making.

We must thus establish institutions and processes that enable scientists both to be credible within politics and to remain worthy of the continuing confidence of the larger society. To achieve this dual goal, the first social responsibility of the scientist remains the integrity of science itself.

Scientists fear that a greater influence on policy will evoke more explicit political control of science. A healthy balance is in the interests of both science and government.

Science and statecraft live in an unresolved crisis. The consequences and power of science, both useful and harmful, are too important to be ignored. Yet the modern state is only beginning to incorporate modern science fully into its daily routines. All branches and levels of government must assert their right to technical information and must develop and maintain the variety of needed institutions and processes.

Many steps should be taken in the organization and decision making of government to enhance the beneficial consequences of science and technology and to avert the unwanted. Among these steps are the following, described in the pages that follow and in the detailed reports of the Carnegie Commission, which are listed in Appendix C.

WHITE HOUSE AND EXECUTIVE OFFICE OF THE PRESIDENT

Science Advice to the President. To serve the direct and immediate needs of the President for scientific and technical advice, the access of the President to science and technology advice should be kept strong through the appointment and utilization of the Assistant to the President for Science and Technology and the President's Council of Advisors on Science and Technology.

Science and Technology in the Executive Office of the President. To keep expertise in science and technology at par with that in national security, economics, and other key fields of White House decision making, the strength of the Office of Science and Technology Policy should be maintained, and technically knowledgeable individuals should be appointed to all relevant organizational units in the Executive Office of the President.

Integration across Policy Areas. To integrate cross-cutting policy motifs, such as environment, energy, and the economy, high-level mechanisms must be strengthened to enhance rational analyses that exhibit clearly tradeoffs, costs, and benefits.

Coordination across the Federal Government in Science and Technology. To provide a high-level forum for the assessment and harmonization of policies relating to science, technology, and research and development, the interagency Federal Coordinating Council on Science, Engineering, and Technology should be convened regularly at cabinet level, with the participation of the Director of the Office of Management and Budget.

CONGRESS

To improve the way members receive and use scientific and technological information, and to enhance the quality of that information, Congress should consider a variety of procedural initiatives, including the establishment of a Congressional Science and Technology Study Conference as a legislative service organization.

JUDICIARY

To improve the quality of scientific and technical information that enters the courtroom and to enhance the capacity of judges and jurors to evaluate and apply it in a legal setting, resource centers should be established within both the scientific community and the federal and state judiciaries, and a nongovernmental Science and Justice Council should be established to monitor and initiate changes that may have an impact on the capacity of the courts to manage and adjudicate cases involving S&T information.

STATES

To bring responsiveness and a broader reach to the making and implementation of policies on the use of science and technology, states should become full partners with the federal government in policy deliberations and be fully represented in advisory mechanisms and decision-making about federal S&T institutions. To help make the partnership effective, the states must enhance their internal resources for science and technology and the mechanisms for interstate and state–federal cooperation; to this end, the states should aim toward the establishment of a national organization that can speak collectively for the states and provide information on state technology activities.

INTERNATIONAL AFFAIRS

To better mesh America's international policies and actions with knowledge of science and technology, the entire Executive Branch of the federal government, particularly the State Department, should take actions at all levels to bring understanding of science and technology to diplomacy.

GLOBAL DEVELOPMENT

To harness more effectively the vast potential of science and technology for cooperative global development, the Administration and Congress should join in passing the first major Foreign Assistance Act since 1961; the Act should create a National Action Roundtable for International Development, bringing together the government, private sector, and not-for-profit nongovernmental organizations in intersectoral coalitions to meet specific challenges.

INTERNATIONAL SCIENCE ADVICE

To assist international decision making by governments and intergovernmental organizations, especially as it relates to the global prospect for sustainable and equitable development, the advisory capability of such international nongovernmental scientific organizations as the International Council of Scientific Unions should be strengthened, along with ways for science advisors to heads of state, and for national organizations such as the National Research Council and the congressional Office of Technology Assessment, to network with their counterparts.

NATIONAL SECURITY

To strengthen and preserve the nation's defense and commercial technology bases in a period of rapidly declining defense budgets, steps must be taken toward their integration; in particular, to make substantial gains in the effectiveness of defense spending and to take advantage of the production efficiencies of U.S. companies competing in world markets, a sweeping reform of the defense acquisition system must be undertaken, involving conversion from a regulation-based to a market-based procurement system and a shift wherever possible from military to commercial specifications.

Economic Performance and the Technology Base

To shape and implement federal policy related to economic performance and the national technology base more effectively, arrangements for technology policy in the Executive Office of the President must be clarified and strengthened, the Department of Commerce must become more technologically sophisticated and capable of forging strong partnerships with business, labor, and universities, and the Defense Advanced Research Projects Agency should be transformed into a national Advanced Research Projects Agency.

Mathematics and Science Education

To strengthen mathematics and science education for children in primary and secondary schools, the Department of Education should lead in systemic change, the National Science Foundation should support improvements in classroom instruction, and the two agencies should integrate their activities to diffuse proven educational innovations.

Environment

To improve environmental decision making, the roles and responsibilities of the Environmental Protection Agency, Departments of Commerce and Interior, and other agencies need to be revised, and new arrangements need to be created so that environmental research and development, monitoring, and assessment programs are integrated and are directed to well-established goals.

Regulation

To help government set and implement coherent regulatory priorities, risk inventories should be compiled and relative risk analyses carried out in the Food and Drug Administration, the Occupational Safety and Health Administration, the Environmental Protection Agency, the Consumer Product Safety Commission, and other regulatory agencies, and their regulatory strategies should be coordinated through a high-level mechanism that can draw effectively on expertise in science and technology.

Nongovernmental Organizations in Science and Technology

To improve public policy studies and design, America's extraordinary population of nongovernmental organizations in science and technology should review their missions and procedures in providing advice to government, should seek creative approaches to focusing their skills and resources through cooperative networks, coalitions, and consortia, and should adopt as their primary mission for the next decade the promotion of policy at the national, state, and local levels to improve precollege science and mathematics education for all citizens.

GOVERNMENT'S TECHNICAL LEADERSHIP

Presidential Appointees. To assure that the most qualified scientists and engineers in the nation serve in the approximately 80 top technical jobs in the Executive Branch that require presidential appointment and Senate confirmation, the White House should improve its ability to recruit scientists and engineers and should work with Congress to reduce counterproductive barriers to public service by consolidation and clarification of conflict-of-interest and other regulations.

Career Federal Scientists and Engineers. To improve the recruitment, retention, and utilization of the more than 200,000 scientists and engineers in direct federal employment, the Office of Science and Technology Policy, the Office of Personnel Management, the Federal Coordinating Council for Science, Engineering, and Technology, and Congress must develop sustained strategies and new mechanisms for following through on federal policies for technical personnel.

LONG-TERM GOALS

To focus on challenges to the nation and on roles its scientists and engineers may play that extend beyond the immediate needs of the next few years, a nongovernmental National Forum on Science and Technology Goals should be established, whose purpose would be to foster national discussion among all major sectors of society on objectives and priorities for future decades and generations.

•••••••

In the next section, Commission leaders distill the findings and recommendations contained in the published reports (see Appendix C) and relate these to current developments.

Joshua Lederberg

THE WHITE HOUSE
SCIENCE & TECHNOLOGY AND THE PRESIDENT

WILLIAM T. GOLDEN
Chairman of the Board
American Museum of Natural History

Beginning with President Truman's action in December 1950 following the outbreak of the Korean War, and strengthened by President Eisenhower in 1957 following Sputnik, the United States pioneered in the creation of a science and technology (S&T) advisory organization to the highest level of government.[1,2] With modifications and a brief erasure, this apparatus continues to function successfully and with broadened scope.[2] The concept has radiated worldwide, and comparable organizations have subsequently been established in all major countries and in more than thirty-five smaller ones.[3]

Before the 1988 Presidential election, the Carnegie Commission on Science, Technology, and Government and other organizations made a number of specific recommendations to encourage the availability to and the utilization of advice on science and technology matters by the President and the top staff of the Executive Branch as important ingredients in the formulation and execution of domestic and

[1] Detlev W. Bronk, "Science Advice in the White House: The Genesis of the President's Science Advisers and the National Science Foundation," *Science,* Vol. 186, pp. 116–21, 11 October 1974. Reprinted in *Science Advice to the President,* William T. Golden, editor (New York: Pergamon Press, 1980); second edition in press (Washington, DC: AAAS Press, 1993).

[2] *Science and Technology Advice to the President, Congress, and Judiciary,* William T. Golden, editor (New York: Pergamon Press, 1988); second edition in press (Washington, DC: AAAS Press, 1993).

[3] *Worldwide Science and Technology Advice to the Highest Levels of Governments,* William T. Golden, editor (New York: Pergamon Press, 1991; Washington, DC: AAAS Press, 1993).

foreign policies over a wide spectrum.[4] These recommendations included:

■ Upgrading the status of the Science and Technology Advisor to Cabinet rank as Assistant to the President for Science and Technology (traditionally called the President's Science Advisor) while continuing concurrently as Director of the statutory Office of Science and Technology Policy (OSTP)

■ Reestablishing the President's Science Advisory Committee (PSAC) of highly qualified outside advisors appointed by the President and chaired by the Science Advisor

■ Filling all of the four presidentially appointed Associate Director positions in the OSTP

■ Revitalizing the Federal Coordinating Council on Science, Engineering, and Technology (FCCSET)

These four recommendations were implemented by President Bush, after some delay, with the appointment of D. Allan Bromley as Assistant to the President for Science and Technology. The consequences have been salutary. PSAC was renamed the President's Council of Advisors on Science and Technology (PCAST). An additional recommendation that Associate Directors of OSTP work part-time with the National Security Council staff and with others in the Executive Office of the President to improve communications and the development and integration of ideas remains for consideration by the Clinton administration.

The prompt appointment by President Clinton of the admirably qualified John H. Gibbons as Assistant to the President for Science and Technology encourages the expectation that the reenergizing of the advisory apparatus under President Bush, so skillfully effected by Dr. Bromley, will be maintained and further strengthened. The relationships, both organizational and personal, among the President, Vice President Gore, and the Science and Technology Advisor, along with the White House staff and other units of the Executive Branch, are in an early stage of evolution. PCAST members and the Associate Directors of the OSTP are yet to be appointed. It is expected that the Science Advisor will have a major influence in these and other S&T-related appointments. Notable among these are the selection of a successor to Walter Massey as Director of the National Science Foundation and of a Director of the National Institutes of Health.

It is hoped that the President will ask the PCAST to address important problems and opportunities requiring science and technology expertise, such as health care, national security, environment, education, and science policy. Through the

---

[4] *Science & Technology and the President,* A Report by the Carnegie Commission on Science, Technology, and Government, pp. 11 + 26. New York, October 1988.

PCAST mechanism, the President can reach out to the entire diversified science and engineering communities for ideas and participation.

Certain closely related by-products of the President's science and technology advisory concept should be mentioned:

■ The establishment in 1991 under the auspices of the Carnegie Commission of the informal "Carnegie Group" (as they call themselves) of science and technology advisors to the heads of the governments of the G-7 countries and Russia and the European Community as proposed in the introductory essay to *Worldwide Science and Technology Advice to the Highest Levels in Governments* has been a great success. Meetings have been held in the United States, the United Kingdom, and France; and semiannual meetings are scheduled in the other member countries, the next to be in Canada in May 1993.

■ Also pursuant to the proposal in the same introductory essay, an initial meeting of science and technology advisors to the top levels of governments of Latin America and other Western Hemisphere countries was convened in November 1991 in Ixtapa-Zihuatanejo under the auspices of President Salinas of Mexico. A second meeting, also in Mexico, is scheduled for June 1993 at Acapulco.

■ In its 1992 report on *Science and Technology in U.S. International Affairs*, the Commission proposed the creation of the position of Counsellor for Science and Technology to the Secretary of State (comparable to the Science and Technology Advisor to the President) with a high-level advisory committee (comparable to PCAST). This recommendation has been strongly endorsed. Strengthening of the status and contributions of science and technology in the State Department in foreign policy development is essential in the world of today and tomorrow. It is hoped that Secretary of State Warren Christopher and the new administration will pay exquisite attention to this long recognised and long neglected issue.

The utility of a science and technology advisory organization for the President has been tested over the years, and its value is increasingly evident as the world changes and as science and technology become more and more pervasive in everyday life. With appropriate modifications, similar S&T advisory mechanisms are developing in the legislative and judicial branches of our federal government and in the states, as well as in foreign countries.

William T. Golden

CONGRESS
SCIENCE, TECHNOLOGY, AND THE LEGISLATIVE PROCESS

JOHN BRADEMAS
President Emeritus
New York University

In the *Federalist* papers, James Madison wrote, "A good government implies two things: first, fidelity to the object of government, which is the happiness of the people, secondly, a knowledge of the means by which that object can be best obtained." Madison's 1788 message holds true today; frequently, "knowledge of the means" requires a strong grasp of highly complex scientific and technological matters. With the rapid rate of current scientific advance and technological innovation, Congress must address a wide range of complex issues.

Although the intricacy of science and technology (S&T) issues complicates the work of Congress, science can also provide keys to the solutions to some of our nation's toughest policy challenges, such as intensified international economic competition, the AIDS epidemic, environmental degradation, and threats to national security. In its first two reports, our Committee on Congress focuses on how Congress receives and uses scientific and technological information. The Committee found many ways in which Congress can improve this process by facilitating more ready access to information and by more effectively using the information that it currently receives. The congressional support agencies (the Congressional Budget Office, the Library of Congress, the General Accounting Office, and the Office of Technology Assessment) are particularly helpful to Congress in evaluating issues with scientific components, and we present a number of suggestions for strengthening their capacity to aid Members of Congress in the decision-making process.

In our third and final report, we evaluate the procedures by which Congress addresses S&T issues and suggest a variety of organizational and procedural reforms. We direct our recommendations towards enhancing procedures for setting long-term goals; strengthening the role of congressional leadership; reorganizing committee structures; shifting to a multiyear budget cycle; reducing earmarking through the use of merit review; and improving the authorization and oversight processes. During my tenure as Majority Whip of the House of Representatives, I experienced firsthand many of the problems this report considers, such as the difficulty of setting budget priorities and the challenge of addressing issues that cut across the jurisdictions of several committees.

Congress is a remarkable democratic institution, and, like the people it represents, it struggles with its imperfections and seeks to operate more effectively. In the light of the recent formation of the Joint Committee on the Organization of Congress, this is an especially opportune time to consider how Congress addresses S&T issues and how its efforts can be made more effective. The dramatically in-

Science and Technology Study Conference and Institute

Key among the Committee's recommendations is the establishment of a Science and Technology Study Conference, a bipartisan congressional organization designed to encourage the informal discussion of science and technology issues that cut across committee jurisdictions. Several Members of Congress have already taken initial steps to organize such a study conference.

The Carnegie Commission is also aiding in the establishment of a nonprofit institute dedicated to promoting the understanding of S&T issues in Congress and to encouraging better communication between the scientific and engineering communities and Congress on public policy issues. The Commission has begun publication of *Science & Technology in Congress*, a monthly bulletin designed to inform Members, congressional staff, and interested individuals outside Congress of the status of S&T issues on and off the Hill. It has also sponsored a series of Member and staff briefings on current S&T issues, such as the future of the Department of Energy's national laboratories, indirect costs and the nation's universities, and women and minorities in science.

creased popularity of the House Committee on Science, Space, and Technology in the 103rd Congress illustrates the growing interest in science and technology among Members of Congress and underscores the timeliness of improving the ways in which Congress deals with S&T issues. We hope that our reports and related activities will prove useful to Congress as it considers innovative ways to use science and technology in responding to the opportunities and challenges of the next century.

John Brademas

JUDICIAL DECISION MAKING
CREATING OPPORTUNITIES AND MEETING CHALLENGES

HELENE L. KAPLAN
Attorney
Skadden, Arps, Slate, Meagher & Flom

Our examination of the courts' capacity to handle complex science-rich cases has occurred at a time of increasingly vocal criticism of the judicial system's ability to manage and adjudicate S&T issues. While acknowledging that problems do exist, the Task Force on Science and Technology in Judicial and Regulatory Decision Making believes that many of the criticisms of our court system stem from misperceptions about the differing methodologies and goals of science and law.

Recent developments in both law and science have conspired to bring increasingly complex scientific issues before the courts for resolution. In particular, the dramatic growth in toxic torts and environmental litigation has put new pressure on the legal system, which is simultaneously being asked to adjudicate issues on the frontiers of science and to develop theories of substantive law. This pressure is intense because of the large numbers of people that are involved and the profound social, economic, and public policy concerns that these new legal claims raise.

While the Task Force's initiatives have begun the process of improving the ability of courts to handle complex S&T issues within the present adversarial system, long-term improvement will require a sustained effort. The Task Force recommends, therefore, the establishment of an independent nongovernmental Science and Justice Council, comprised of lawyers, scientists, and others outside the judiciary, to monitor and initiate changes that may have an impact on the ability of the courts to manage and adjudicate S&T issues. It would also address such fundamental problems as the lack of adequate data about the incidence and management of S&T issues in litigation; judicial access to scientific assessments; and the alternatives to judicial resolution of complex S&T cases.

A centerpiece of the Task Force's efforts has been the creation of a judicial reference manual that outlines the wide range of techniques that judges have used for managing S&T issues. The manual is nearing completion in cooperation with the Federal Judicial Center; it will be widely disseminated to federal judges and then throughout the state court system. Models for protocols have also been created, jointly with members of the S&T community, in the areas most frequently encountered in litigation such as toxicology, epidemiology and (bio)statistics. These protocols provide questions to aid the decision-making process regarding challenges to expert testimony based on (a) the qualifications of experts, (b) the validity of the theory on which the expert is relying, (c) the reliability of the data underlying the theory, and (d) the sufficiency of the expert's opinion to sustain a verdict.

Our court system's reliance on expertise managed by the litigants is exacerbated by the lack of any resources within the judiciary that would assist judges in their adjudication of S&T issues. This institutional void is being addressed, in part, by a new S&T research and education program within the Federal Judicial Center. Recommended by the Task Force, and initially funded by Carnegie Corporation of New York, the program will update and maintain the judicial reference manual, de-

Scientific "Facts" and the Judicial System

Scientists view their work as a body of working assumptions, of contingent and sometimes competing claims. Even when core insights are validated over time, the details of these hypotheses are subject to revision and refinement as a result of open criticism within the scientific communities. Scientists regard this gradual evolution of their theories through empirical testing as the pathway to "truth."

In the legal system, however, all of the players are forced to make decisions at a particular moment in time, while this scientific process is going on. Given the indeterminacy of science, how can the judicial system make the best use of a scientific "fact"? This question is at the core of the Judicial Task Force's efforts.

velop judicial education programs, identify needed research, and encourage outreach with the scientific and judicial communities.

In addition, the Task Force has served as a catalyst for initiatives undertaken by the American Bar Association/American Association for the Advancement of Science National Conference of Lawyers and Scientists, the Brookings Institution, and the Institute for Civil Justice of the Rand Corporation. The Task Force has also developed a pilot judicial education program to familiarize judges with scientific methodology.

The increasing number of new categories of S&T cases entering the courts before science has adequately explored the issues that will be relevant to judicial decision making makes this a particularly opportune time to address these issues. Wisdom counsels action now.

Helene L. Kaplan

STATES
MEETING NATIONAL CHALLENGES THROUGH A STATE–FEDERAL SCIENCE AND TECHNOLOGY PARTNERSHIP

RICHARD F. CELESTE
Former Governor
State of Ohio

The Carnegie Commission's task forces have devoted themselves to America's great contemporary challenges. Among the priorities considered have been industrial competitiveness, environmental protection, and education—the common thread in each being science and technology. Another thread, less obvious, but no less critical, is the role of the states in addressing each of these challenges. State governments, working with industry and academia, have evolved fresh approaches in all of these areas. They hold the seeds of striking innovation on a national scale. Such a role for the states, though, runs counter to two generations of tradition: since the Second World War, largely for reasons of national security, the balance of effort in applying science and technology to national needs has tilted heavily toward the federal government. The end of the Cold War brings this nation the opportunity, and the necessity, to strike a new balance, more suited for the great challenges of today. This new balance, closer to that envisioned by the Framers of our Constitution, will allow the nation to achieve more effective and direct response to these issues. This opportunity underscores the historic role of the states as sources of vigor and innovation, in the great constitutional tradition of self-renewal.

The Commission has recommended that the states should be full partners with the federal government in meeting these challenges by applying science and technology. States should be represented in federal policy deliberations, both in setting priorities and in designing programs that share state and federal resources.

States should be represented on federal advisory committees at all levels, from the highest national policymaking councils to individual research laboratories. States should also be partners in defining new missions and new modes of operation for federal science and technology institutions, especially the federal laboratories.

To create the partnership, the states will have to take a number of steps on their own. First, they must establish a national organization that can speak collectively for them and provide information on state technology activities. A congressionally sanctioned interstate compact, much like the Education Commission of the States, was recommended by the Commission. In the interim, before a compact can be fully enacted, an organization that expands on the activities of the Science

State Technology Programs: The Lessons Learned

Since the early 1980s, nearly every state has developed a technology program of some kind. The majority of state programs foster business-driven partnerships between industries and universities, among the best-known being the Ben Franklin Partnership in Pennsylvania and the Thomas Edison Program in Ohio.

Several important lessons have been learned from the experience gained in Ohio. First, build on local or regional strengths. The challenge is to ensure that these industrial sectors are globally competitive. Second, let the private sector set the investment decision. Successful centers tend to have industry-dominated boards and count on industry funds for a substantial portion of their budget. Third, invent new partnerships that create a cooperative environment for academic researchers, small business people, and others who may not be used to working with each other. Fourth, recognize that small and medium-sized firms (the ones that cannot afford their own R&D capabilities) are the biggest customers for the application of new knowledge to products and production processes. Often, training is an essential component of "diffusion" or "extension." There are two other important lessons of the state experience. One is that capital and management capability as well as technology are often required. The second is that every investment faces the "whisper of the guillotine." These are often high-risk ventures—and rules and understandings need to be established in order to recognize failure early, both with innovative companies and with technology centers.

SCIENCE, TECHNOLOGY, AND GOVERNMENT FOR A CHANGING WORLD

and Technology Council of the States, an arm of the National Governors Association (NGA), will be needed.

State governments will need to bolster their own sources of information and analysis. Each governor should appoint a science and technology advisor to act as a focal point for advice on the full range of scientific and technological issues that governors face. Each state needs to have an independent science and technology advisory body to provide objective analysis and advice to both governors and legislators faced increasingly with technological decisions.

A number of steps are being taken to implement the Task Force's recommendations. NASA is sponsoring, in conjunction with the Commission and the NGA, a two-part effort to follow up on the report. The first element is a State–Federal S&T Colloquium that will bring together one individual from each state, chosen by the governor, with key federal agency staff and Clinton Administration technology staff. The Colloquium will shape specific proposals for cooperation between the states and federal agencies. In such a setting, the complex issues of a true partnership can be deliberated and refined into concrete action items, as part of a national economic competitiveness strategy. The second element will be a compendium of information on state technology initiatives, featuring a detailed case study on each program and an analysis of the broad issues facing the states. The lack of such information is often cited as the major obstacle frustrating state–federal cooperation. We expect that the Department of Commerce and perhaps the Defense Advanced Research Projects Agency will join NASA in sponsoring this initiative.

Presentations of the report are also being made in individual states, at regional state meetings, and through organizations such as the National Governors Association and the National Council of State Legislators.

Richard F. Celeste

INTERNATIONAL AFFAIRS
SCIENCE AND TECHNOLOGY IN U.S. INTERNATIONAL AFFAIRS

RODNEY W. NICHOLS
Chief Executive Officer
New York Academy of Sciences

The international relations of the United States have suffered from the absence of a long-term, balanced strategy for issues at the intersection of science and technology with foreign affairs. This absence of analysis and policy leads to unpreparedness for major issues, bitter interagency disputes, and inadequate last-minute preparations for international negotiations.

Moreover, serving the *domestic* interests of the United States in the 1990s calls for sharply improved incorporation of scientific and technological insight into the nation's international policies. Goals in trade, defense, and energy, as well as in health, agriculture, telecommunications, environment, space, and other critical fields, all call for integrating domestic and international considerations. In turn, the analyses of national options for these goals demand the most recent and reliable scientific knowledge available from worldwide sources.

To make matters even more complex, the likely continued scarcity of human and financial resources, along with the remarkable new worldwide opportunities for political and economic cooperation, combine to underscore the importance of forming more international partnerships. Broadening international alliances already include the research, development, and education conducted by many U.S. universities and firms, while government has lagged. Yet, government must play its influential role in orchestrating the pace, rules, and prospects for success of partnerships linking the U.S. public and private sectors for essential work with both developed and developing countries.

Examples of the growing number of international S&T issues

- The opportunity for further trade in products and services—computers, telecommunications, pharmaceuticals, and aircraft, for example—will be decided in such forums as the General Agreement on Tariffs and Trade (GATT).
- Our future peace depends on successful negotiations in reducing the number of weapons of mass destruction and the successful monitoring of these agreements using sophisticated surveillance systems.
- The international movement of hazardous waste is increasingly controlled through international agreements such as the Basel Convention.
- The intellectual property rights of U.S. inventors need to be protected overseas.
- "Big Science" projects (for example, nuclear fusion research, environmental monitoring, and the program for mapping and sequencing the human genome) are increasingly shared international projects.

In the Executive Branch over many years, however, there has been a crazy-quilt of poorly defined responsibilities for science and technology in international affairs. Agencies have inconsistent strategies and inadequate resources. Programs are frequently knotted up with conflicting policies, erratic funding, and micromanagement. Only rarely are efforts properly knitted together, and then only by *ad hoc* mechanisms of coordination. The results have been poor, hardly befitting America's extraordinary assets in science and technology, and the consequences have been frustrating to Congress as well as to the President and the Secretary of State.

The most important task in the near term is to clarify the international responsibilities and priorities for S&T among the mission agencies and to ensure their overall coordination with foreign policy. A White House review should be undertaken in order to gather the information and establish the framework for presidential decisions and consultations with Congress. Starting with an urgent Presidential request to all agencies, a comprehensive inquiry will lead to sharper designation of selected lead-agency responsibilities for implementing programs, operating under White House and State policy control. State must strengthen its commitment to science and technology and must concentrate on foreign policy formulation and review, ensuring consistency in the complex settings for the conduct of U.S. foreign affairs. In parallel, Congress must sort out its priorities and jurisdictions.

Despite the astonishing growth of *both* competition and cooperation in science and technology around the world, many crucial international programs are "orphans" in the federal agencies—from energy and AIDS to intellectual property standards and environmental cooperation. So immediate attention must be given to clearing away the fogs of ambiguity that surround each agency's international roles. Top officials in the White House Office of Science and Technology Policy, the National Security Advisor's staff, the National Economic Council, the State Department, and mission agencies, as well as the many House and Senate committees concerned with foreign affairs involving science and technology, must all develop the habit of working closely together to rethink objectives and pursue informed global programs.

Overall, there are three aims for the mid-1990s: to define afresh the U.S. international goals in and for S&T; to bring the increasingly important international programs into the mainstream *throughout the S&T agencies of the government*; and to orchestrate use of the nation's full technical assets, especially from the private sector, in order to fulfill the goals of American foreign policy. Put another way, the urgently needed presidential and congressional decisions must integrate national policies *for* international S&T and must bring the nation's best S&T *to* foreign policy.

Rodney W. Nichols

GLOBAL DEVELOPMENT
COOPERATION FOR DEVELOPMENT CAN PREVENT SOMALIAS

Jimmy Carter
Former President of the United States

Although we have sent troops to Somalia, we are sobered to realize that Sudan, Bangladesh, Sri Lanka, Mozambique, Liberia, Haiti, Angola, Burma, and almost two dozen other nations also cry out for international assistance to find peace or food. Civil wars usually develop when neighbors contend for dwindling supplies of food, water, arable land, or a modicum of human dignity. Freedom, justice, and human rights are usurped by the powerful with weapons, to whom these concepts are meaningless or anathema.

International troops cannot be rushed to all war-torn and starving countries to preserve fragile cease-fires or to control warlords who postpone looting until foreign soldiers depart. Timely assistance is often the answer here, not troops. Most international aid agencies and bilateral programs are nearly 50 years old. Their own leaders acknowledge that huge bureaucracies are delivering assistance with appalling inefficiency. Realizing this, those of us with wealth to share have become increasingly averse to doing so. In America, "foreign aid" is becoming a profane phrase, almost politically suicidal for a member of Congress to utter approvingly.

This has led to neglect. The facts are truly disturbing. In 1990, $880 billion was spent worldwide on weapons and preparations for war, 15 times the total of all non-private development assistance. Military purchases by the poorest nations have quintupled in the past three decades, so that they are now almost triple humanitarian aid received. Amazingly, only 7% of bilateral assistance and less than 10% of multilateral aid is for education, health, clean water, shelter, sanitation, family planning, and nutrition.

Third World foreign debt skyrocketed during the 1980s. When I left the White House, there was a net transfer of about $35 billion annually from industrialized to less developed nations. Now, mostly for servicing debt, the net flow is $60 billion from the poorest to the richest countries. The most destitute people labor and exhaust their mines and forests in vain. Total annual exports of Somalia, Mozambique, and Sudan will not service their debt.

Despite its great need, Africa has been hit especially hard in the loss of development assistance. Compared with 1990, aid from all countries in 1991 declined $1.3 billion (11%), finances from the World Bank group dropped $600 million (15%), and soft development loans (International Development Agency) fell by $780 million (60%). International Monetary Fund Loans plunged 42%. This lost support is particularly counterproductive in the increasing number of countries moving from war to peace and from despotism to democracy. European countries respond best to these needs, with France and the Scandinavian countries giving from 0.25% to 0.36% of their gross domestic product in aid to Africa in 1990. (The U.S. contributed 0.02%.)

Part of the problem is with the aid organizations. Hundreds of well-intentioned international agencies, with their own priorities and idiosyncrasies, seldom cooperate or even communicate with each other. Instead, they compete for publicity, funding, and access to potential recipients. Overburdened leaders in developing countries, whose governments are often relatively disorganized, confront a cacophony of offers and demands from donors.

Since its inception in 1961, the U.S. Agency for International Development's effectiveness has been diminished in two major ways. First, a disproportionate number of staffers are based in Washington, rather than in developing countries. Fewer than 38% are career development officers, and more than half of these are in Washington. Second, some 80% of all "economic support funds" are spent in Egypt and Israel alone. Further, Congress micromanages the agency's budget, earmarking nearly two-thirds of all "development assistance" funds, thus allowing virtually no flexibility for the agency to direct money where it is needed.

Against the background of these problems, which I publicized in a recent *Wall Street Journal* article (December 29, 1992), the Carnegie Commission's Task Force on Development Organizations made a comprehensive set of recommendations. Among the most important are:

- The White House must take the lead. The President must articulate anew the

Follow-up to the Task Force on Development Organizations

n December 1992, President Carter and UN Secretary General Boutros Boutros-Ghali brought together leaders of private lending and donor organizations, officials of developing countries, and representatives of the Bush administration, Congress, and the Clinton transition team to evaluate the ideas of the Carnegie Commission Task Force on Development Organizations. Arising from the conference were a number of recommendations and commitments to improve coordination of development assistance, both financial and technical, that can be a foundation of a new "preventive diplomacy."

principles and long-range priorities for cooperation with the entire range of developing countries. Concurrent with new presidential leadership, Congress should initiate broad consultations, studies, and hearings that will lead to a major reform of "foreign assistance" legislation and oversight.

■ To fulfill its mandate, the Agency for International Development (AID) must increase its access to American science and technology, enhance staff skills, decentralize authority, improve long-term planning, and match its organization to evolving international conditions. More generally, the means for interagency program development must be strengthened.

■ A National Action Roundtable for International Development (NARID) should be created, with balanced representation from the private, governmental, and independent sectors, to foster creative cooperation among U.S. institutions.

■ Above all, greatly enhanced means must be devised internationally for coordinating the ongoing efforts of major donors.

With strong support from the White House, the United Nations, and other key donors, these reforms can be implemented. Only then will we see sustainable development adequate to prevent future Somalias.

Jimmy Carter

INTERNATIONAL SCIENCE ADVICE

THE INSTITUTIONS OF SCIENCE AND THE GLOBAL PROSPECT:
THE CASE OF ENVIRONMENT

THOMAS F. MALONE
Department of Marine, Earth, and Atmospheric Sciences
North Carolina State University

K nowledge is the driving force of human progress. Our capacity to generate, integrate, disseminate, and apply knowledge will determine the human prospect in the 21st century.

This is the central issue in addressing the environmental *problematique* that has attracted growing worldwide attention during the past decade. The Earth Summit in Rio de Janeiro in June 1992 profoundly and irreversibly changed the nature of that *problematique* by combining it with the issue of economic development.

Rio deepened the focus from the *manifestations* of environmental changes in the air, land, water, and plant and animal kingdoms to the *causes* of those changes. These are found in the conversion of planet Earth's natural resources into goods and services to satisfy human needs and wants. Knowledge gains during the 20th century have dramatically increased individual capacity to effect this conversion.

Striking asymmetry in knowledge and in its use result in poverty and environmental degradation in some parts of the world and in such high production and consumption in other parts that the stability of the global environment is placed in jeopardy. These circumstances complicate the pursuit of a world in which the basic needs and an equitable share of the wants of everyone are met in a healthy, physically attractive, and biologically productive environment.

To help sustain a fair, green, productive world, science itself must change, it must spread, and it must develop new partnerships. Increased emphasis is necessary on the *integration* of knowledge through interdisciplinary studies that embrace the natural, social, and engineering sciences and the humanities. New efforts must be mounted to improve the *dissemination* of knowledge globally through formal and informal education. New modes for the *application* of knowledge must be forged through collaboration among business and industry responsible for the production of goods and services, governments responsible for the commonweal, and academia as the prime generator, disseminator, and custodian of knowledge.

To address the combined knowledge needs of environment and development and to link knowledge with policymaking in fields such as climate change, desertification, and biodiversity require establishment of a global network of interdisciplinary and intersectoral institutions. We propose the formation by donor organizations of an international Consultative Group for Research on Environment (CGREEN) to foster and support this network.

To provide rigorous, balanced, scientific assessments on issues of environment and development for governments, international governmental organizations, and the private sector, international nongovernmental organizations with competence in the natural, social, and engineering sciences must enhance their capabilities and clarify the procedures they follow to formulate advice. Foremost among the

Environmental Lessons of the Past Twenty Years

- The burdens placed on the environment and the resources of knowledge and money at our disposal to modify and adjust these burdens contest endlessly.

- Simply keeping pace with environmental demands is likely to become harder.

- People everywhere are demanding higher environmental quality.

- Environmental issues are increasingly shared and international.

- Developing countries are most at risk from environmental problems.

- The need for international action with respect to the environment is particularly pressing because of the potential conflict between economic advance in developing countries and protection of the environment.

SCIENCE, TECHNOLOGY, AND GOVERNMENT FOR A CHANGING WORLD

nongovernmental organizations that can play an enhanced role in provision of international science advice to governments is the International Council of Scientific Unions.

On a governmental level the emergence of networks of science advisors to heads of government holds great promise for cooperative and collective action, not only in environment and development, but in all fields where science, technology, and government interact.

Creation of international institutional arrangements to pursue the many dimensions of environmental knowledge and to link them with policy is a paramount challenge for the 1990s. The stage is set for action.

Thomas F. Malone

NATIONAL SECURITY

NEW THINKING AND AMERICAN DEFENSE TECHNOLOGY

WILLIAM J. PERRY*
Chairman & Chief Executive Officer
Technology Strategies & Alliances, Inc.

F our major factors will drive defense policy during the 1990s in dramatically different directions from those that it took during the four decades of the Cold War.

■ A discontinuity has occurred in world affairs. With the move of the Soviet Union to create democratic institutions and enter the world market system, the Cold War has ended; with the dissolution of the Warsaw Pact and the disintegration of the Soviet Union, the reemergence of a military threat from the former Soviet Union seems remote. With the disappearance of this threat, the U.S. defense budget has declined 25% in the past five years, and will probably decline an additional 25% in the next five years.

■ A less sudden but comparably profound change has taken place in the global technology base. In the United States, defense now accounts for less than a third of R&D spending, down from its previously dominant role. At the same time, R&D investments by America's commercial competitors have grown rapidly, so that U.S. defense now funds less than a ninth of the R&D in the Western industrialized world—whereas it used to fund one-third. In fact, in some fields crucial to defense (microelectronics, for example) defense is a minor player.

■ A dramatically increased appreciation of the decisive role of technology in mod-

* This contribution was prepared before Dr. Perry's nomination to serve as U.S. Deputy Secretary of Defense.

ern warfare has taken place. The overwhelming victory in Desert Storm, and the minimal casualties suffered by coalition forces, was paced by the first application of the "offset strategy," a new military technology developed by the United States, originally intended to "offset" the numerical advantage of Warsaw Pact forces.

■ The well-documented problems with U.S. defense acquisition, which have plagued us for many years, are coming to be seen as intolerable, particularly in the light of increasing production efficiencies being developed by U.S. companies in order to be competitive in world markets.

These factors are so significant that they demand "new thinking" in U.S. defense policy. The National Security Task Force of the Carnegie Commission has focused its efforts these past three years on assessing what new defense policies are required, particularly with respect to American defense technology. The findings of the Task Force are summarized in two reports: *New Thinking and American Defense Technology,* August 1990, and *A Radical Reform of the Defense Acquisition System,* December 1992.

The principal recommendation of the Task Force is that the country's defense industry should be integrated with its commercial industry to form a single indus-

The Importance of Dual-Use Technologies

For technologies of broad use to society as well as defense (for example, information technologies) the message is clear: Defense systems will incorporate newer and better technology if they use technology spawned in the commercial sector. But DoD has the technological instincts and habits of a technology leader that develops all the technology it needs—instincts and habits formed in earlier decades of technological dominance. To be sure, in fields where commercial and military needs are technically different, DoD can and must rely on its own R&D rather than on the commercial sector's. But elsewhere, the barriers to technology sharing between the commercial and defense sectors are purely nontechnical. These barriers include burdensome government contracting and accounting procedures, military security and proprietary restrictions, and unnecessary military specifications. These barriers must be lowered if DoD is to have access to the latest commercial technology.

SCIENCE, TECHNOLOGY, AND GOVERNMENT FOR A CHANGING WORLD

trial base. This radical change would allow the introduction of major efficiencies in defense acquisition, would remove the principal impediment to defense contractors' converting to commercial products during the downsizing of defense, and would facilitate the reconstitution of a major defense production capability if a superpower military threat were to arise at some future time.

Several specific recommendations are subsumed in this broad recommendation:

■ Maintain defense's contribution to the national technology pool by sustaining defense spending on technology base (6.1 and 6.2 programs) and technology demonstrators (6.3a programs), at the expense of full-scale development and production programs.

■ Broaden the charter of the Defense Advanced Research Projects Agency (DARPA) to include responsibility for stimulating the diffusion of dual-use technology to commercial applications, and change its name to ARPA (that is, drop the exclusive emphasis on defense technology).

■ Replace milspec (military specification) standards with dual military–industrial standards, which will be guided primarily by industrial needs whenever commercial applications dominate the market.

■ Convert the defense acquisition system from a regulation-based system to a market-based system.

■ Create a Presidential Commission, patterned after the "base-closing" commission, to recommend the necessary changes in acquisition law and agency mandates, including the phasing down of agencies and government laboratories where necessary.

William J. Perry

ECONOMIC PERFORMANCE
ORGANIZING THE EXECUTIVE BRANCH FOR A STRONGER NATIONAL
TECHNOLOGY BASE

ADMIRAL B.R. INMAN
United States Navy (Retired)

I mproved national economic performance requires sustained growth in pro-
ductivity. The development and diffusion of new technology and its underlying science have been a major source of such growth. The federal government
has contributed to technological growth, indirectly through economic policies, and
directly as a part of traditional government investment in defense, space, health,
science and agriculture. Dramatic changes in this process have occurred in recent
years as American commercial manufacturing leadership has declined, increased international economic interdependence has developed, and a separation has steadily
grown between a fast-moving commercial technology base and an increasing decline in Department of Defense leadership in the creation of new technology.

Primary responsibility for the advance and use of commercial technology rests
with the private sector. But the federal government can do more to assist in many
ways, and it must act to halt the deterioration of the defense technology base. As
investment in defense steadily declines, it becomes increasingly mandatory that the
federal government act to help create a single integrated technology base for the
country. Changes in organizational structure to ensure the development of coordinated policies are essential if success is to be achieved.

The Carnegie Commission has focused its recommendations on the development and coordination of coherent technology policies in the Office of the President and on expanding the role of existing agencies in the pursuit of technolo-

gies that offer substantial promise for commercialization and the creation of additional U.S. jobs.

Within the Office of the President, the Science Advisor, operating with the support of the Office of Science and Technology Policy, is the key to improved performance in the development and coordination of new technology policies. He needs to reach out beyond the government to pull in the best advice available within the country and to marshal the best efforts of the departments and agencies of the Executive Branch. Additional analytical support for his effort is required, and this probably can be effectively supplied by the newly created Critical Technologies Institute.

Coordination of the developed policies, allocation of adequate resources, and oversight of execution by the departments and agencies needs to function daily at the direction of the President. The Commission had recommended that the National Security Council fulfill this role in the absence of other mechanisms, but readily accepts the new National Economic Council as the prospective vehicle to perform the required tasks for the President.

To move rapidly toward creation of a single national technology base, the Commission recommended an expanded role for the Advanced Technology Program at the National Institute of Standards and Technology and transformation of the Defense Advanced Research Projects Agency to provide stronger links between

The Changing Economic Landscape

Three major changes have occurred in recent years. First, American commercial manufacturing leadership has eroded in many sectors—particularly in the automotive, electronic, and semiconductor industries—at the same time that growth in the world technology base and the globalization of industrial activities have increased international economic interdependence. Second, in fast-moving dual-use fields (those with both commercial and defense applications), the Department of Defense has gone from being a technological leader to a follower, as commercial demands for increasingly complex components determine research and development priorities. Third, the commercial technology base has become more and more inaccessible to the military technology base, in part because of complex military accounting and procurement policies and in part because commercial research and development have grown much more rapidly.

SCIENCE, TECHNOLOGY, AND GOVERNMENT FOR A CHANGING WORLD

modern military needs and high-technology commercial industry. The Commission proposed changing the name of DARPA to the National Advanced Research Projects Agency as a start toward helping create a national, rather than solely a defense, technology base. In introducing legislation to enact this proposed expansion in mission, Senator Jeff Bingaman proposed an elegant solution of simply dropping the word "Defense" from the Agency's title, returning to its origin as the Advanced Research Projects Agency. The important decision that has not yet been made is to accelerate use of the Agency's competence in the pursuit of dual-use technologies that have potential commercial payoff.

EDUCATION

IN THE NATIONAL INTEREST: THE FEDERAL GOVERNMENT
IN THE REFORM OF K–12 MATH AND SCIENCE EDUCATION

LEWIS M. BRANSCOMB
Albert Pratt Public Service Professor
Science, Technology, and Public Policy Program, John F. Kennedy School of
Government, Harvard University

Public education in America is primarily a state and community responsibility. It has failed to prepare all our young people for productive lives and good citizenship. While the federal government provides only 6 percent of the funding for this system, it is committed to lead a national effort, in partnership with the states, to upgrade the system of public education.* Both student performance and teacher preparation are particularly inadequate in mathematics and science. For this reason, and because the federal government engages half the nation's R&D effort, a federal priority for math and science education is appropriate.

Many barriers impede rapid progress. Too many children come to school ill-prepared to learn. Too few teachers are properly trained in math and science, and too many work in regimented, demotivated environments. Too few parents realize that the schools are not challenging their children to reach their potential. Too many Americans believe that you must be gifted to learn math and science; in fact, everyone can learn. Hard work, not innate talent, is the key to learning.

Why have past federal efforts yielded so little progress?

---

* The President and the governors pledged their joint efforts to ambitious national education goals at the summit meeting in Charlottesville, Virginia, in October 1988, ending a political debate about whether there was a legitimate role for the federal government in school reform.

The Carnegie Commission found the federal effort divided and incoherent. The Department of Education (DoEd) was addressing systemic problems largely through formula grants with little discretion to mobilize educational innovations from outside government. The National Science Foundation (NSF) was demonstrating new ideas in curriculum, instruction, and teacher training with little capability to transfer successful experiences into the nation's schools. Both were trying to help the states improve education without good data, without a system model, and with minimum coordination.

Too many Americans believe that you must be gifted to learn math and science; in fact, everyone can learn. Hard work, not innate talent, is the key to learning.

The Commission urged a fivefold federal strategy. Good progress has already been made on a number of elements of the strategy:

■ To change both the ways schools are organized and run and to change what goes on inside the classroom, the Commission urged that NSF and DoEd negotiate a formal agreement to concert their activities. An agreement to effect this collaboration was implemented in 1992.

■ To leverage state and private initiatives for change, the Commission urged that DoEd be given more flexibility to support innovative ideas from outside government. Congress responded by substantially expanding the discretionary portion of the Eisenhower program in math and science.

■ To build a well-informed, broadly participatory collaboration toward shared goals among all concerned parties, in and out of government, the Commission proposed a strong effort in systems research and measurement for understanding what works and monitoring progress, and a variety of institutional mechanisms to create a consensus strategy for reform.

■ To engage the talents and resources of all the federal agencies whose missions depend on technically trained people, and the teachers who educate them, the Commission urged that all of the federal R&D agencies devote a designated percentage of their R&D resources to their participation in that consensus strategy. One percent of federal R&D would more than double the current federal investment in K–12 math and science education.

■ To ensure that all schools can take advantage of the most successful innovations, the Commission urged a substantial effort, using the resources of the National Research and Education Network, in educational extension services, retraining teach-

Complacency Is a Major Pitfall

The most likely path to failure, and ultimately to the destruction of the American dream, is not what happens in DoEd, NSF, or even the statehouses and school board offices. It is the complacency of too many American parents who are unaware that their children's future is at risk, the myopia of too many retired Americans who do not understand that poor schools threaten their safety and social security, and social conditions that result in too many children entering school unprepared. Most unfortunate is the tragic message our current system sends to young women, minorities, and the poor: you haven't the talent to master mathematics and science, so you shouldn't even try.

ers and helping them adopt the best teaching materials and methods arising from advances in cognitive science and learning research.

Most of all, this effort needs a presidentially led, bipartisan commitment for the two or more decades it takes for a new generation of better-educated Americans to make their way through a greatly improved educational process.

Lewis M. Branscomb

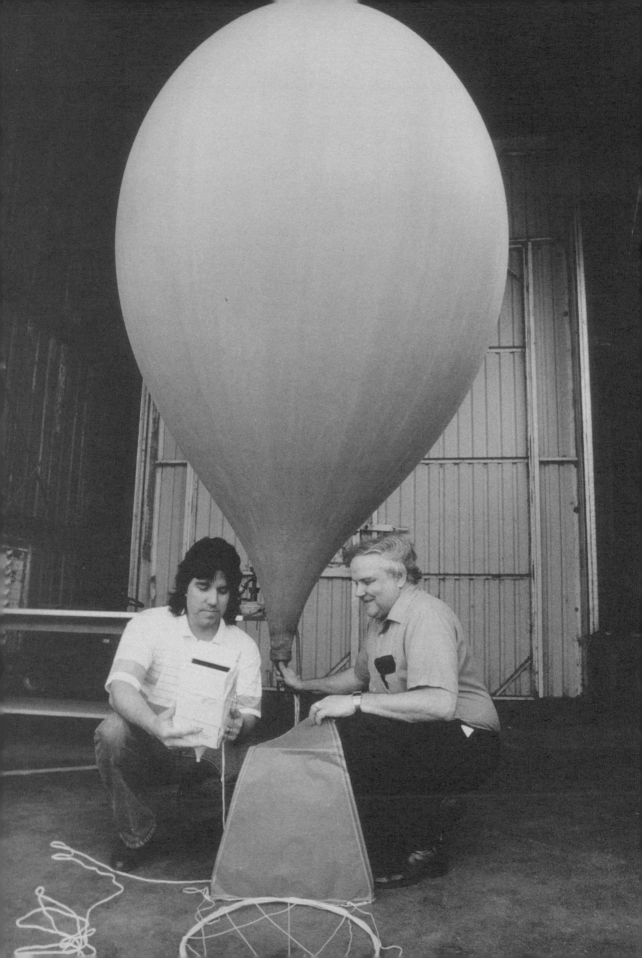

ENVIRONMENTAL RESEARCH AND DEVELOPMENT

STRENGTHENING THE FEDERAL INFRASTRUCTURE

H. Guyford Stever
Former Director
National Science Foundation

Robert Fri
President
Resources for the Future

Over the past three decades considerable progress has been made in recognizing the seriousness of the world's environmental problems, and many positive steps have been undertaken to ameliorate them, yet we are only beginning to understand the complexities of the challenges on the horizon. Our ability to respond to the environmental and economic challenges of today and tomorrow strongly depends on the quality of the information produced by a well-organized and productive federal research and development system.

At first glance, the federal environmental research system seems impressive. More than a dozen federal departments and agencies conduct or sponsor environment-related R&D totaling $5 billion each year. However, the existing federal environmental research programs were built for another time and for a set of issues that no longer correspond to today's environmental priorities. And because this system has developed piecemeal over a number of decades, it is now a collection of diffuse, substantially uncoordinated environmental R&D programs. If the federal government is to provide the scientific resources and leadership that a national and global environmental protection effort requires, a careful examination and rethinking of our R&D effort is essential.

To create a more modern and effective system, the Carnegie Commission's report *Environmental Research and Development: Strengthening the Federal Infrastructure* recommends, among other measures, strengthening and streamlining the current R&D infrastructure, stronger leadership in the Executive Office of the President, encouraging multidisciplinary research efforts, and improving coordination among research programs.

The report recommends integrating the activities of the Council on Environmental Quality into the White House Office of Environmental Quality (OEQ).* A reinvigorated OEQ should look across all departments and agencies and assure that environmental considerations are incorporated into all federal policies. OEQ should also develop broad environmental, sustainable development, and risk-related policy options for the consideration of the President and the Cabinet. To aid the OEQ director, we recommend establishing an Institute for Environmental Assessment to evaluate global and national environmental problems and develop alternative approaches to them.

Our ability to respond to the challenges of today and tomorrow depends on the quality of the information produced by the federal R&D system.

To devise and implement an integrated R&D plan, we also recommend that the President undertake an Environmental Research and Monitoring Initiative to establish a common policy framework for all federal environmental R&D programs, coordinate the diverse activities of federal departments and agencies, and heighten the priority of environmental R&D across the government.

Monitoring, surveying, and evaluating the state of the environment are critical to our national environmental protection efforts. It is important to bring federal activities in this area under one roof. We call for the establishment of a new federal agency, the U.S. Environmental Monitoring Agency (EMA), to be organized by combining the National Oceanic and Atmospheric Administration with the U.S. Geological Survey. EMA's mission would include monitoring and evaluation of both natural processes and the social activities that are driving forces for environmental deterioration.

Within the Environmental Protection Agency (EPA), we recommend consolidating the twelve existing national laboratories into four major national laboratories, and we suggest establishing up to six major Environmental Research Institutes associated with academic institutions and nongovernmental organizations around the country. These institutes would be EPA's flexible, problem-oriented,

* Recently, President Clinton announced his intention to replace the three-member Council on Environmental Quality with an Office of Environmental Policy (OEP).

The Key Role of Environmental R&D

The nation will be able to deal much more effectively with environmental problems once they are better understood. Our ability to understand earth processes and human dynamics is determined by what research is conducted, how it is organized, and how well it is assessed and presented in establishing and implementing environmental policy. And our ability to identify, control, prevent, and clean up pollutants is limited by the effectiveness of the technologies we develop and our ingenuity in finding sound means of promoting the widespread adoption of those technologies. Environmental problems pose a special challenge to the world's scientific and engineering communities, one that evokes the image of the first human step on the moon: Can scientists and engineers generate the kind of large-scale and highly focused effort that took us into space and apply it to developing the understanding necessary to protect our global environment?

multidisciplinary arm, while the national laboratories would maintain their more structured, discipline-oriented, intramural identity.

This is a critical period in the evolution of the nation's environmental programs. Decisive action is needed to ensure that the government can anticipate and respond not only to the challenges that the nation and the world face today, but also to those that are likely to arise in the years ahead.

REGULATION
IMPROVING REGULATORY DECISION MAKING

DOUGLAS M. COSTLE
Former Administrator
U.S. Environmental Protection Agency

One of the most important emerging roles of government in the last 20 years has been the regulation of escalating environmental, health, and safety risks arising from our ever growing and more complex national and global economies. So profound has this growth been that we have already begun to observe significant alteration in the natural balance of global ecological systems. Indeed, the rate of change (as Thomas Malone has pointed out) may be outstripping our ability to assess and advise. Yet, for the most part, environmental policy has tended to be inwardly focused, reactive, and fragmented, as each new problem has driven us into playing "catch up, clean up."

Preoccupied with trying to clean up after the fact the polluting side effects of 20th-century technologies conceived largely in ignorance of their individual and cumulative environmental impacts, we are only now fully realizing that the new imperative is to begin shaping the technologies of the 21st century to achieve a different result.

We argue for strengthening the capacity of the Executive Office of the President to reach out across a fragmented government to begin reformulating policies toward a more sustainable future. The White House is the only place in the federal government that allows a sweeping overview of the regulatory landscape, and is for this reason the best spot from which to view—and repaint—the big picture. The White House must take a fresh look at the underlying premises of a wide variety of functions and activities that government is involved with, including industrial technology, agriculture, transportation, and trade, and reshape them to assimilate the goal of sustainable development. Environmental, economic, and national security policies are inextricably entwined, and institutional arrangements in the Executive Office must incorporate this understanding.

Even as government prepares to respond to the challenges of the future, it must do better at dealing with the legacy of the 20th century. Toward this end, strategic planning must become a core value not only in the Executive Office of the President but in the agencies themselves. The absence of goals, benchmarks, and performance measurement can lead to the perception, sometimes justified, that regulatory programs are adrift among competing interests without clear purpose. While it is incumbent upon Congress and the Executive Office to specify destinations

Interbranch Risk Forum

A central theme in the Task Force's report is the need for sustained dialogue between representatives of the executive, legislative, and judicial branches of the federal government. Too frequently discussions between the branches occur only in rigid adversarial contexts such as hearings. More off-the-record communication focused on broad issues, rather than specific decisions, could help each branch develop realistic expectations about the capabilities and responsibilities of the other branches.

Toward this end, the Task Force is sponsoring a pilot project in conjunction with the Brookings Institution which will bring together ten top officials from each of the three branches for a private and informal colloquy on risk management. These discussions are modeled after Brookings' highly successful Administration of Justice seminars, which convene high-level participants from Congress, the Department of Justice, and the Judiciary.

The high stakes, endemic uncertainty, and complex nature of the administrative process make risk management a particularly fitting topic for such a forum. If the participants consider this initial experience a success, we hope that the risk management forum will become an annual event.

clearly, the agencies will be left to determine the shortest route to get from here to there, and to help ensure that they stay on course.

The agencies must also assume responsibility for much of the job of regulatory coordination. The White House's limited resources coupled with the sheer number of issues it faces limit its ability to ensure regulatory coherence. We recommend the creation of a "Regulatory Coordinating Committee" to serve as a forum for voluntary coordination at the agency level.

The rulemaking process is another area where we need to break the gridlock. Here again our approach in recent years has been reactive, focusing on the end of the system. Too often agencies have spent hundreds of person-years and hundreds of thousands of dollars assembling a rule, only to have it quashed in the end by reviewers in the Executive Office or in the courts. Opportunities for earlier intervention by reviewers need to be created so that corrections can be made before the die is cast.

Our world poses environmental, health, and safety threats of increasing magnitude. At the same time, the potential for poorly crafted regulatory strategies to have deleterious effects on the economy is increasing. There is some good news: the dichotomy between a healthy environment and a vibrant economy is, in theory, false. The bad news is that without major changes in our policies and practices, the dichotomy will become real. To avoid hard choices that we do not have to make, we must quickly change our course and be prepared to readjust it frequently as we learn more. Regulatory institutions must also adapt as circumstances change.

NONGOVERNMENTAL ORGANIZATIONS
THE NEW DIMENSION IN THE RELATIONS BETWEEN SCIENCE AND GOVERNMENT

WILLIAM D. CAREY
Senior Consultant
Carnegie Corporation of New York

When governments trip over dilemmas of scientific uncertainty on the way to making policy or regulatory choices, they tend, these days, to look for help beyond the battling interest groups by seeking impartial advice from nongovernmental organizations (NGOs) with tested *bona fides*. What are the kinds, quality, objectivity, and utility of the advice they variously serve up to governments?

The Task Force of the Carnegie Commission looking into these questions was startled to discover the number and variety of nongovernmental institutions making up an apparently ever-expanding universe of exempt organizations meeting the tests of Section 501(c)(3) of the federal tax code. Within that universe, "scientific and technical" NGOs similarly show both high birth-rate and longevity characteristics, although precise counting of this population is afflicted by serious semantic and classification hazards. The Task Force estimates a cohort of S&T NGOs numbering between two thousand and four thousand.

We are dealing with a segment of the voluntary sector, an open system enabling individuals with multiple interests to affiliate with nonprofit professional or advocacy organizations whose purposes and methods they find meritorious. Gross "bean counting" leads to an eye-popping individual member estimate of 16 million. Correction for multiple memberships would likely deflate that reading to a few million. Moreover, the profusion of S&T-type NGOs disguises enormous differences in breadth, financial viability, roles, missions, and levels of comfort and skill in working with governments.

The evidence is strong that government is seeking and getting increasing streams of technical inputs from NGOs. Much of it comes from the mainstream scientific and technical professional organizations, which can deliver experts and study panels from their member pools, or can absorb a share of the torrent of agency and committee requests for data-gathering and complex analytic research. But smaller, newer, and creatively led NGOs respond as well, often with less baggage than the slower-paced establishment groups.

A dominant feature of the NGO movement, including its scientific subset, is its pluralism. All shades of purpose, mission, and perception of the roles of science and technology are found in an organizational universe insisting upon self-governance and autonomy. Coherence does not follow naturally from that predisposition. The sciences are often heard to speak in discordant tongues when political decision makers encounter the NGOs.

The combination of autonomy and pluralism is reassuring as a form of checks and balances, but this reassurance is offset to some degree by the costs of what former Carnegie Corporation president John Gardner terms "extravagant pluralism."

The Task Force sought to examine the flows of services and connections between NGOs and government from the viewpoints of each party to the relationship. Volume is one measure of the health of the arrangements, and not necessarily what matters most. Government asks hard questions of NGOs, and for the most part good ones, yet is somehow myopic when it comes to investing in underlying policy analysis assets and capacity. NGOs speak to government on varying wavelengths, sometimes as authoritative representatives of the sciences, at other times as advocacy or quasi-advocacy organizations with policy predispositions. It is small wonder when NGOs and government talk past each other. Yet this does not diminish government's appetite for NGO support nor NGO zeal for a voice in complex problems of choice.

In its report, *Facing Toward Governments: Nongovernmental Organizations and Scientific and Technical Advice*, the Task Force aims its principal recommendations at the governing bodies of the scientific and technical NGOs, stressing the vital needs of trustees to monitor the independence, objectivity, and accountability of the organization's interactions with government—legislatures, executive branches, courts, and regulatory regimes. It calls for more NGO capacity-building for policy research, and for commensurate government reinvestment in analytic resources. It reminds NGOs that advice isn't necessarily a good business for every NGO.

The NGO universe can approach closer to its potential as a source of disinterested

Nongovernmental Organizations: An Extremely Diverse Group

The nongovernmental organizations (NGOs) studied include those societies, associations, academies, and institutes with primary memberships of scientists, engineers, and researchers; Internal Revenue Service 501(c)(3) tax-exempt status, which severely limits overt lobbying activities; a strong interest in providing rigorous technical input to government decision making; and independent, often elected, governing bodies.

NGOs range from broad-spectrum general-purpose scientific and technical groups, such as the American Association for the Advancement of Science, to elite academies, such as the National Academy of Sciences and its affiliated National Research Council, from there to an extensive array of discipline-specific societies, such as the American Physical Society, through think tanks dedicated to government work, such as the RAND Corporation, and on to policy advocacy groups, such as the World Resources Institute.

and valuable counsel to governments, including state and local governments along with international bodies. The leaderships of the concerned organizations should create and test coordinating arrangements that would permit mutual assistance in research, greater coherence in representing the sciences, and strengthening of government's level of confidence in the existence of shared NGO standards of objectivity, accountability, and quality assurance in supplying advice and technical support.

The scale, advancing expertise, and surging vitality of S&T NGOs mark a telling shift in the way government and science have looked at each other since World War II and through the years of the Cold War. It no longer reflects the textbook three-dimensional model of interaction among government, industry, and the research universities. The growth, "clout," and repositioning of the NGOs in relation to government's mounting and sometimes intransigent dilemmas of science and technology all point to the NGO sector as a *de facto* fourth dimension in an altered model—a dimension holding every promise for larger roles for the voluntary sector in shaping public interest outcomes.

William D. Carey

GOVERNMENT'S TECHNICAL LEADERSHIP
ASSURING SCIENTIFIC COMPETENCE IN PUBLIC SERVICE

NORMAN R. AUGUSTINE
Chair & Chief Executive Officer
Martin Marietta Corporation

M any of the most critical issues the nation will face in the next decade are steeped in science and technology content: the environment, competitiveness, health care, national security, energy, and the physical infrastructure—to name but a few. The federal government's capacity to deal effectively with these issues will depend to a considerable degree upon the quality of scientific and technological personnel having responsibilities in these areas.

The ability of the federal government to obtain and retain the needed individuals can be considered in two distinct categories: presidential appointees and the federal career service. Approximately 80 key policy positions appointed by the President and confirmed by the Senate are normally held by scientists and engineers. In the case of the career workforce, approximately ten percent of all federal employees are engaged in scientific and engineering pursuits, and the federal government is the largest employer of scientists and engineers in the United States.

There is growing evidence, however, that many high-quality scientists and engineers are no longer attracted to government service. The time required to fill key positions is increasing, and the fraction of candidates expressing a willingness to serve is declining. Although the challenges of attracting top-quality personnel are substantial in any field, they are particularly acute in the scientific and engineering disciplines because in these fields government service frequently is not viewed as career-enhancing. In addition, there is a severe shortage of women and minorities in the technological disciplines, thereby further limiting the available talent reservoir. In the case of presidential appointees, the pool of experienced candidates is yet again reduced, particularly in the instance of specialists in national security matters, by the fact that the federal government is the largest or, in some cases, the sole potential client for the services of such individuals after they complete their federal service—thus heightening conflict-of-interest ramifications.

Although the actions needed to alleviate these difficulties are as diverse as the reservations expressed by potential employees—the latter ranging from concern over job satisfaction and the ability to carry out key programs to a widely perceived decline in the esteem of public service—two actions appear to offer considerable promise, one relating to career employees and one to presidential appointees.

Recent legislation affecting the career service workforce has in fact been helpful and now needs to be fully implemented—but so too does true pay reform. Career government service must offer overall remuneration generally comparable to alternative forms of employment in the private sector and should include considerable flexibility to recognize location, specialty, and, above all, performance. In the case of presidential employees, in most cases it is not practicable or necessary to seek to match the income potential that this caliber of individual might enjoy in the private sector. On the other hand, certain other impediments to government service could be removed, such as well-intentioned but overly restrictive and vague conflict-of-interest regulations.

The existing set of rules and laws needs to be consolidated into a single, clear

Reducing Hurdles and Disincentives

To ensure clear understanding and more effective enforcement, the government's ethics laws should be streamlined and clarified as soon as possible, and they should be contained in a single comprehensive section of the U.S. Code. They should then be evaluated periodically for their impact and effectiveness in ensuring ethical conduct with as little negative effect on recruitment and retention of scientific and engineering personnel as possible. Overlapping laws should be repealed immediately.

statement based on banning inappropriate post-employment behavior rather than post-employment itself. Further, a functioning mechanism is needed for providing written "safe harbor" opinions for departing employees seeking counsel; individuals from academia should in general not be expected to relinquish tenure; and certain categories of financial conflicts should be dealt with by recusion rather than divestiture.

Given the minuscule number of individuals with science or engineering background who serve either in elective office or in the highest level appointee positions, it is particularly important that those positions which are in fact filled by scientists and engineers draw from the most highly qualified individuals in the nation. If this is to be the case, much remains to be accomplished with regard to federal personnel policies.

Norman R. Augustine

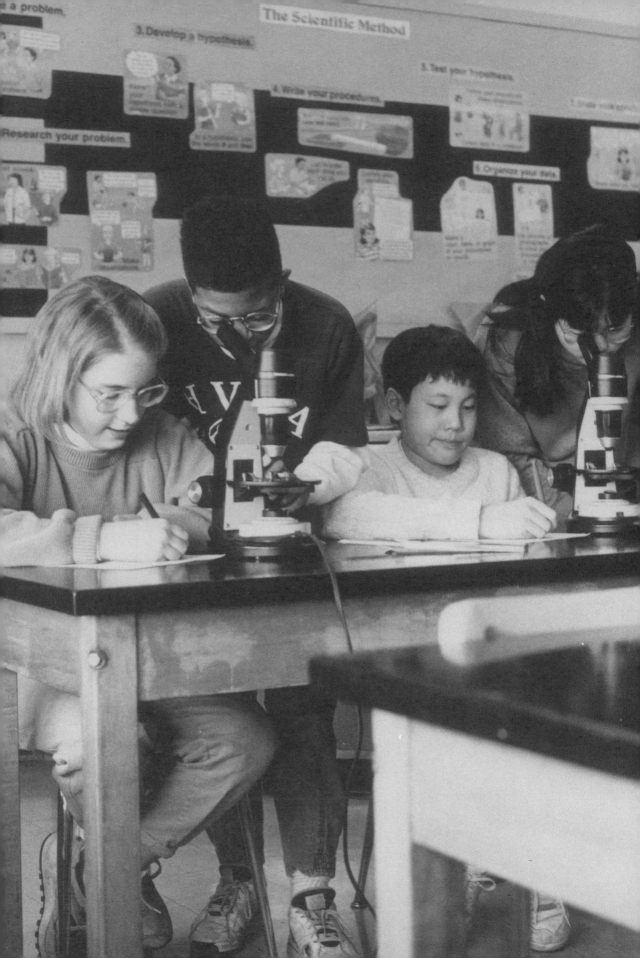

LONG-TERM GOALS

LINKING SCIENCE AND TECHNOLOGY TO SOCIETAL GOALS

H. GUYFORD STEVER
Former Director
National Science Foundation

Today, with the historic opportunities presented by the dramatic world events of recent years, the United States has a great need to address a broad range of societal goals, focusing more attention on human, social, and economic concerns. Science and technology are fundamental to enabling society to achieve these goals. Devoting more attention to the long-term dimension of science and technology policy is critically important in today's rapidly changing, highly competitive global economy. Directing our resources to a clearly articulated set of goals is essential if the United States is to enjoy a new age of vitality and leadership in the world.

In *Enabling the Future: Linking Science and Technology to Societal Goals*, we outline recommendations designed to encourage longer-term thinking about the role of science and technology in our society. Within the federal government, we propose mechanisms for institutionalizing long-term science and technology goal-setting as an integral part of the policymaking and budgeting processes in the legislative and executive branches. Outside government, we suggest the involvement of all major sectors of society in an ongoing dialogue on future directions for science and technology in the context of societal goals.

All major sectors of society—government, industry, academia, nongovernmental organizations, and the public—have key roles to play in the process of set-

An example of an activity of the National Forum is an effort to articulate long-term goals related to the technology development required to achieve our environmental quality objectives, including the sustainable use of resources. What are the environmental and resource problems we are likely to encounter in the decades ahead? What technologies will enable us to explore the nature of these problems? What technologies will help us prevent or mitigate the problems we face? How can we bring these new technologies to the global marketplace? What federal government funding and programmatic changes are needed to assist in answering the questions above? These are the kinds of questions a National Forum should try to answer.

ting long-term science and technology goals. Scientists alone cannot develop these goals; a coordinated effort by a cross-section of society is essential. We must clearly articulate the potential contributions of science and technology to a broad range of major societal goals such as public health and human development, a competitive economy, sustainable use of natural resources, and national security. Such an effort must also ensure a solid science and technology base, including facilities and education and research programs. Only with such a robust, resilient science and technology base can both the predictable advances and the unexpected breakthroughs in science and engineering be integrated effectively into organized efforts to achieve societal goals.

A major recommendation of our report is that a nongovernmental National Forum on Science and Technology Goals be formed to facilitate the exchange of policy ideas and to define science and technology goals in the context of national and international goals. We have received a very positive response to this recommendation and have already made strides toward its implementation. The National Academy of Sciences is interested in hosting the Forum, and the Carnegie Commission is working with the Academy to develop an organizational plan and to obtain seed funding.

H. Guyford Stever

APPENDIX A

ABOUT THE CARNEGIE COMMISSION ON SCIENCE, TECHNOLOGY, AND GOVERNMENT

The Carnegie Commission on Science, Technology, and Government was established by Carnegie Corporation of New York in 1988. Its charter was described by Carnegie Corporation president David A. Hamburg:

> The main purpose of the Commission is to seek ways in which the branches of government can encourage and use the contributions of the national scientific community. The nation needs more effective mechanisms, both governmental and nongovernmental, for analyzing thoroughly and objectively what science can do for society and how society can make sure that scientific and technological capabilities are humanely used.

The Commission is an independent bipartisan body. About half the members of the Commission and its Advisory Council are scientists or engineers who have had experience in government or close association with government agencies. The remaining members are individuals with broad experience in society and government who have worked closely with scientists. Appendix B lists the Commission and Advisory Council members.

The Commission's mandate has been broad. It has focused on topics where we believe there is receptivity for fundamental change in the institutions involved; where the recommendations could have long-term impact; where the Commissioners and Advisory Council members have considerable, and in some cases unique, expertise; and where other organizations are not pursuing similar goals, for example, health care.

In pursuing its mandate, the Commission has sponsored special studies, seminars, and workshops and has contracted with scientific organizations and outside consultants. Its major activities, however, have been the work of its task forces and special committees (see Appendix C). About twenty Commission reports have been issued, as well as a number of Commission-sponsored publications by outside groups. Commission reports (see Appendix C) may be obtained from the Commission's headquarters at 10 Waverly Place, New York, NY 10003, until July 1, 1993; after that date, reports may be obtained from Carnegie Corporation of New York, 437 Madison Avenue, New York, NY 10022.

APPENDIX B
COMMISSION AND ADVISORY COUNCIL

CARNEGIE COMMISSION ON SCIENCE, TECHNOLOGY, AND GOVERNMENT

William T. Golden (Co-Chair)
Joshua Lederberg (Co-Chair)
David Z. Robinson
   (Executive Director)
Richard C. Atkinson
Norman R. Augustine
John Brademas
Lewis M. Branscomb
Jimmy Carter
William T. Coleman, Jr.
Sidney D. Drell
Daniel J. Evans
Andrew J. Goodpaster
Shirley M. Hufstedler
B. R. Inman
Helene L. Kaplan
Donald Kennedy
Charles McC. Mathias, Jr.
William J. Perry*
Robert M. Solow
H. Guyford Stever
Sheila E. Widnall
Jerome B. Wiesner

---

* Through February 1993

ADVISORY COUNCIL

Graham T. Allison, Jr.
William O. Baker
Harvey Brooks
Harold Brown
James M. Cannon
Ashton B. Carter
Richard F. Celeste
Lawton Chiles
Theodore Cooper
Douglas M. Costle
Eugene H. Cota-Robles
William Drayton
Thomas Ehrlich
Stuart E. Eizenstat
Gerald R. Ford
Ralph E. Gomory
Theodore M. Hesburgh
Walter E. Massey
Rodney W. Nichols
David Packard
Lewis F. Powell, Jr.*
Charles W. Powers
James B. Reston
Alice M. Rivlin †
Oscar M. Ruebhausen
Jonas Salk
Maxine F. Singer
Dick Thornburgh
James D. Watkins ‡
Herbert F. York
Charles A. Zraket

---

* Through April 1990
† Through January 1993
‡ Through January 1989

APPENDIX C
TASK FORCES AND REPORTS

EXECUTIVE OFFICE OF THE PRESIDENT

Science & Technology and the President (October 1988)
- This first report of the Commission calls for strengthening the science and technology expertise available to the President and the Executive Branch by expanding the role of the Office of Science and Technology Policy and by elevating the position of Science Advisor to Assistant to the President for Science and Technology.

"Strengthening the Policy Analysis and Research Role and Capability of the Office of Science and Technology Policy, Executive Office of the President," Background Paper, William G. Wells, Jr., and Mary Ellen Mogee (May 1990)

"The Budget Process and R&D," Consultant Report, Willis H. Shapley (April 1992)

COMMITTEE ON SCIENCE, TECHNOLOGY, AND CONGRESS

John Brademas (Chair)	Daniel J. Evans
Jimmy Carter	Charles McC. Mathias, Jr.
Lawton Chiles	H. Guyford Stever

Kathryn L. Edmundson (Assistant to Commissioner Brademas)

Science, Technology, and Congress: Expert Advice and the Decision-Making Process (February 1991)
- This report reviews and recommends changes in the mechanisms used by Congress to obtain expert science and technology advice. The report calls for the creation of a bipartisan "Science and Technology Study Conference" to coordinate among congressional committees handling S&T issues and for the establishment of a private nonprofit "Science and Technology Study Institute" to facilitate communication between Congress and the scientific and engineering communities.

Science, Technology, and Congress: Analysis and Advice from the Congressional Support Agencies (October 1991)
- This report recommends a range of improvements in the analytical capabilities of the four congressional support agencies: the Office of Technology Assessment, the Congressional Research Service of the Library of Congress, the General Accounting Office, and the Congressional Budget Office.

Science, Technology, and Congress: Organizational and Procedural Reforms (expected June 1993)
- This third and final report of the Committee on Congress will offer recommendations to improve internal congressional organization and procedures for dealing with science and technology issues—particularly with respect to budget, authorization, and appropriations processes.

Working With Congress: A Practical Guide for Scientists and Engineers, William G. Wells, Jr., sponsored by the Carnegie Commission on Science, Technology, and Government and the American Association for the Advancement of Science, AAAS Press (December 1992)

TASK FORCE ON SCIENCE AND TECHNOLOGY IN JUDICIAL AND REGULATORY DECISION MAKING

Helene L. Kaplan (Chair)
Alvin L. Alm
Richard E. Ayres
Sheila L. Birnbaum
Stephen G. Breyer
Harry L. Carrico
Theodore Cooper
Douglas M. Costle
E. Donald Elliott
Kenneth R. Feinberg
Robert W. Kastenmeier
Donald Kennedy
Francis E. McGovern

Richard A. Merrill
Richard A. Meserve
Gilbert S. Omenn
Joseph G. Perpich
Paul D. Rheingold
Maurice Rosenberg
Oscar M. Ruebhausen
Pamela Ann Rymer
Irving S. Shapiro
William K. Slate, II
Patricia M. Wald
Jack B. Weinstein

Margaret A. Berger, Senior Consultant

Science and Technology in Judicial Decision Making : Creating Opportunities and Meeting Challenges (March 1993)
■ Recent developments in law and science have combined to bring increasingly complex scientific issues before the courts for resolution. This report recommends the preparation of a Reference Source for judges, increased science education for judges, the development of institutional linkages to allow judges easier access to scientific information in the courtroom, and the establishment of a non-governmental Science and Justice Council to monitor and initiate changes that may have an impact on the courts' ability to manage and adjudicate S&T issues.

New Frontiers in Regulatory Decision Making: The Role of Science and Technology (April 1993)
■ This report focuses on how science and technology are used in developing risk-related policy and attempts to identify potential reforms. The report recommends that the Executive Office of the President take a proactive role in providing broad policy guidance to regulatory agencies and avoid micromanagement of policy details.

"The Work of the Federal Courts in Resolving Science-Based Disputes: Suggested Agenda for Improvement," Report of a Working Group (1989); reprinted in *Federal Courts Study Committee Working Papers and Subcommittee Reports,* Vol. 1 (July 1, 1990)

"Procedural and Evidentiary Mechanisms for Dealing with Toxic Tort Litigation: A Critique and Proposal," Consultant Report, Margaret A. Berger (October 1991)

Brief of the Carnegie Commission on Science, Technology, and Government as *Amicus Curiae* in Support of Neither Party, *Daubert v. Merrill Dow Pharmaceuticals, Inc.,* No. 92-102, In The Supreme Court of the United States (December 2, 1992).

■ The Carnegie Commission filed this *amicus curiae* brief with the Supreme Court of the United States in a case concerning standards for admissibility of S&T expert testimony. The brief proposes an integrated approach to scientific evidence that acknowledges and respects both the special expertise of science and the judge's responsibility to declare law. This brief builds on the work of the Task Force although it is not a product of the Task Force.

TASK FORCE ON SCIENCE AND TECHNOLOGY AND THE STATES

Richard F. Celeste (Chair)
William O. Baker
Arden L. Bement, Jr.
Erich Bloch
Lawton Chiles
Daniel J. Evans
B. R. Inman

H. Graham Jones
Frank E. Mosier
Walter H. Plosila
Donna Shalala
Luther Williams
Linda S. Wilson
Charles E. Young

Christopher M. Coburn (Assistant to Governor Celeste)

Science, Technology, and the States in America's Third Century (September 1992)

■ This report calls for a stronger state role in science and technology policy, recommending the formation of an interstate compact to coordinate S&T activities among states. The report recommends that each state appoint both a science advisor to the governor, and a science and technology advisory board to the legislature.

INTERNATIONAL STEERING GROUP

Rodney W. Nichols (Chair)
Harvey Brooks
Victor Rabinowitch

Walter A. Rosenblith
Jesse H. Ausubel (rapporteur)

SCIENCE AND DIPLOMACY REVIEW PANEL

Rodney W. Nichols (Chair)
Harry G. Barnes, Jr.
Justin Bloom
Harvey Brooks
Kenneth H. Keller

Victor Rabinowitch
Walter A. Rosenblith
Eugene B. Skolnikoff
John Temple Swing
John C. Whitehead

Science and Technology in U.S. International Affairs (January 1992)

■ Emphasizing that foreign affairs must be seen in the context of S&T in every branch and level of the government, this report recommends strengthening the State Department's capability to deal with science and technology issues as they relate to foreign affairs. The report calls for the appointment of a Science and Technology Counselor to the Secretary of State, and for an increase in the number of science and technology officers working at embassies abroad.

"The United States as a Partner in Scientific and Technological Cooperation: Some Perspectives from Across the Atlantic," Consultant Report, Alexander Keynan (June 1991)

Task Force on Development Organizations

Jimmy Carter (Chair)	John P. Lewis
Rodney W. Nichols (Vice Chair)	Lydia Makhubu
Anne Armstrong	M. Peter McPherson
Harvey Brooks	Rutherford M. Poats
John R. Evans	Francisco Sagasti
Robert W. Kates	George P. Shultz, Jr. (Senior Advisor)

Maryann Roper (Assistant to President Carter)
Patricia L. Rosenfield (Carnegie Corporation of New York liaison)

Partnerships for Global Development: The Clearing Horizon (December 1992)

■ Emphasizing that science and technology are among the most powerful tools for international development, this report recommends the establishment of a National Action Roundtable for International Development to catalyze the creation of public–private coalitions to address critical development problems. Recommendations for change within the U.S. Agency for International Development are also explored.

"The United States and Development Assistance," Background Papers for the Task Force on Development Organizations, Susan U. Raymond, Charles Weiss, Edgar C. Harrell, and David Mosher (June 1992).

Multilateral Issues Review Panel

Thomas F. Malone (Chair)	Victor Rabinowitch
John Ahearne	Walter A. Rosenblith
Jesse Ausubel	Eugene B. Skolnikoff
Harvey Brooks	H. Guyford Stever
Philip Hemily	David G. Victor
Rodney W. Nichols	Gilbert F. White

International Environmental Research and Assessment: Proposals for Better Organization and Decision Making (July 1992)

■ This report emphasizes the need to strengthen worldwide cooperative capabilities for environmental research and assessment. Calling for the creation of a new multilateral institution to meet this goal, a Consultative Group for REsearch on ENvironment (CGREEN), the report urges the U.S. Government to take the lead in forging international environmental cooperation.

AD HOC TASK FORCE ON NATIONAL SECURITY

William J. Perry (Chair)*	Joshua Lederberg
Norman R. Augustine	Rodney W. Nichols
Lewis M. Branscomb	David Packard
Harold Brown	H. Guyford Stever
Ashton B. Carter	Sheila E. Widnall
Sidney D. Drell	Jerome B. Wiesner
William T. Golden	R. James Woolsey*
Andrew J. Goodpaster	Herbert F. York
B.R. Inman	Charles A. Zraket

*Through February 1993

New Thinking and American Defense Technology (August 1990)

■ This report examines the role of science and technology in the post–Cold War era, recommending major changes in the operations and decision-making processes of the national security establishment. The report calls for strengthening the Defense Science Board and establishing a high-level national security science and technology advisory panel in the White House.

■ Supplementary report. "A Radical Reform of the Defence Aquisition System" (December 1992).

TASK FORCE ON SCIENCE, TECHNOLOGY, AND ECONOMIC PERFORMANCE

B.R. Inman (Chair)	Robert A. Frosch
Norman R. Augustine	William G. Howard, Jr.
Lewis M. Branscomb	Philip A. Odeen
Daniel Burton	William J. Perry
Ashton B. Carter	Robert M. Solow
Theodore Cooper	Elmer B. Staats
Edward E. David	

Technology and Economic Performance: Organizing the Executive Branch for a Stronger National Technology Base (September 1991)

■ This report presents a compelling argument for organizational changes that will help move the United States toward a single dual-use (commercial and military) technology base. Among other recommendations, the report calls for transforming the Defense Advanced Research Projects Agency (DARPA) into a National Advanced Research Projects Agency (NARPA).

Task Force on K–12 Mathematics and Science Education

Lewis M. Branscomb (Chair)
Bill Aldridge
Richard C. Atkinson
Garrey E. Carruthers
Eugene H. Cota-Robles
Shirley M. Hufstedler
David Kearns

Leon M. Lederman
Shirley M. McBay
Lauren B. Resnick
F. James Rutherford
Roland W. Schmitt
Maxine F. Singer
Sheila E. Widnall

Rollin Johnson (Assistant to Commissioner Branscomb)
Vivien Stewart (Carnegie Corporation of New York Liaison)

In the National Interest: The Federal Government in the Reform of K–12 Math and Science Education (September 1991)

■ Recognizing that math and science education serve as a foundation for the future economic success of the nation, this report recommends that the Department of Education and the National Science Foundation formally coordinate their efforts to improve science and math education in the United States.

Task Force on Environment and Energy

H. Guyford Stever (Chair)
Robert W. Fri

Edward A. Frieman
Gordon J. F. MacDonald

E3: Organizing for Environment, Energy, and the Economy in the Executive Branch of the U.S. Government (April 1990)

■ Recognizing the interrelation between environment, energy, and the economy, this report recommends instituting a mechanism within the Executive Branch for integrated policy analysis of these three issues. The report emphasizes coordination of research among Executive Branch agencies, and strengthening the State Department's capability to analyze and respond to foreign policy implications of issues in environment and energy.

Task Force on the Organization of Federal Environmental R&D Programs

Robert W. Fri (Co-Chair)
H. Guyford Stever (Co-Chair)
Douglas M. Costle
Edward A. Frieman
Stephen J. Gage

Bruce W. Karrh
Gordon J. F. MacDonald
Gilbert S. Omenn
Gilbert F. White

Environmental Research and Development: Strengthening the Federal Infrastructure (December 1992)
■ This report discusses ways in which the distribution of environmental R&D responsibilities throughout the government can be reorganized. Among other recommendations, the report calls for the consolidation of the EPA's laboratory structure, and the establishment of six major Environmental Research Institutes.

TASK FORCE ON NONGOVERNMENTAL ORGANIZATIONS

Charles McC. Mathias (Co-Chair)
William D. Carey (Co-Chair)
Oakes Ames
Anne W. Branscomb
Harvey Brooks
Mary E. Clutter
Edward E. David
William Drayton
Lilli S. Hornig

Richard A. Meserve
Charles W. Powers
Paul G. Rogers
Elspeth D. Rostow
John E. Sawyer
Marcia P. Sward
F. Karl Willenbrock
Charles A. Zraket

Facing Toward Governments: Nongovernmental Organizations and Scientific and Technical Advice (January 1993)
■ Recognizing that the government increasingly turns to independent organizations for expert science and technology advice, this report recommends that NGOs review their missions and objectives with respect to policy processes in the government. The report calls on NGOs to adhere to the scientific processes of critical review and open argumentation.

"The Role of NGOs in Improving the Employment of Science and Technology in Environmental Management," Background Paper, Charles W. Powers (May 1991)

PERSONNEL: SCIENTISTS AND ENGINEERS IN THE FEDERAL GOVERNMENT

Mark Abramson
Ernest Ambler
Norman R. Augustine
William O. Baker
Alan K. Campbell
William T. Coleman, Jr.
Kenneth W. Dam
John M. Deutch
Alan E. Fechter (Staff, NRC)
John S. Foster, Jr.
Robert A. Frosch
E. Pendleton James

William M. Kaula
Stephen J. Lukasik
Lawrence McCray (Staff, NRC)
Michael McGeary (Staff, NRC)
G. Calvin MacKenzie
John P. McTague
Howard Messner
Rodney W. Nichols
Janet L. Norwood
James Pfiffner
Alan Schriesheim
Charles Schultze

Robert L. Seamans, Jr.
Linda S. Dix Skidmore (Staff, NRC)
Bruce L. R. Smith
John F. Trattner

J. Jackson Walter
Anne Wexler
R. James Woolsey*
James B. Wyngaarden

* Through February 1993

Recruitment, Retention, and Utilization of Federal Scientists and Engineers, Alan K. Campbell and Linda S. Dix, eds., National Academy Press, Washington, DC, 1990.

The Prune Book: The 60 Toughest Science and Technology Jobs in Washington, John H. Trattner, Madison Books, Lanham, MD, 1992.

Improving the Recruitment, Retention, and Utilization of Federal Scientists and Engineers, A. Campbell and S. Lukasik, co-chairs, National Academy Press, Washington, DC, 1993.

Science and Technology Leadership in American Government: Ensuring the Best Presidential Appointments, K. Dam, chair, National Academy of Sciences, National Academy of Engineering, National Institute of Medicine, Committee on Science, Engineering, and Public Policy, National Academy Press, Washington, DC, 1992.

Task Force on Establishing and Achieving Long-term S&T Goals

H. Guyford Stever (Chair)
Harvey Brooks
William D. Carey
John H. Gibbons

Rodney W. Nichols
James B. Wyngaarden
Charles A. Zraket

Enabling the Future: Linking Science and Technology to Societal Goals (September 1992)
■ This report outlines policy changes designed to encourage longer-term thinking about S&T goals both within and outside government. The report recommends forming a nongovernmental National Forum on Science and Technology Goals to facilitate the definition and monitoring of long-term S&T goals.

■■■■■■

A Science and Technology Agenda for the Nation: Recommendations for the President and Congress (December 1992)
■ This report summarizes Commission recommendations on the economy, national security, environment, science education, and the White House.

APPENDIX D
PARTICIPANTS IN COMMISSION ACTIVITIES
WITH THEIR AFFILIATIONS

Mark Abramson
President
Council for Excellence in
    Government

John Ahearne
Executive Director
Sigma Xi

Bill Aldridge
Executive Director
National Science Teachers
    Association

Graham T. Allison, Jr.
Douglas Dillon Professor of
    Government and Director,
    Strengthening Democratic
    Institutions
John F. Kennedy School of
    Government
Harvard University

Alvin L. Alm
Director
Science Applications International
    Corp.

Ernest Ambler
Director Emeritus
NIST

Oakes Ames
Empire State Fellow
New York Academy of Sciences

Anne Armstrong
Chairman of the Board of Trustees
Center for Strategic and
    International Studies

Jeannette L. Aspden
Managing Editor
Carnegie Commission on Science,
    Technology, and Government

Philip Aspden
Independent Consultant

Richard C. Atkinson
Chancellor
University of California, San Diego

Norman R. Augustine
Chair & Chief Executive Officer
Martin Marietta Corporation

Jesse H. Ausubel
Director of Studies
Carnegie Commission on Science,
    Technology, and Government

Richard Ayres
Attorney
O'Melveny & Myers

William O. Baker
Former Chairman of the Board
AT&T Bell Telephone Laboratories

Harry G. Barnes, Jr.
Director General, Emeritus
Foreign Service

David Z. Beckler
Associate Director
Carnegie Commission on Science,
    Technology, and Government

Arden L. Bement, Jr.
Basil S. Turner Distinguished
    Professor of Engineering and
Director of Midwest
    Superconductivity Center
Purdue University

Jonathan Bender
Program Associate
Carnegie Commission on Science,
    Technology, and Government

Margaret A. Berger
Professor of Law and Associate Dean
Brooklyn Law School

Sheila L. Birnbaum
Attorney
Skadden, Arps, Slate, Meagher
    & Flom

Bonnie P. Bisol
Office Manager, Washington Office
Carnegie Commission on Science,
    Technology, and Government

Erich Bloch
Distinguished Fellow
Council on Competitiveness

Justin Bloom
Consulting Engineer
Technology International

John Brademas
President Emeritus
New York University

Anne Branscomb
Research Affiliate
Harvard University

Lewis M. Branscomb
Albert Pratt Public Service Professor
Science, Technology, and Public
    Policy Program
John F. Kennedy School of
    Government
Harvard University

Stephen G. Breyer
Chief Judge
U.S. Court of Appeals for
    the First Circuit

Harvey Brooks
Professor Emeritus of Technology
    and Public Policy
Harvard University

Harold Brown
Counselor
Center for Strategic and
    International Studies

Daniel F. Burton
Executive Vice President
Council on Competitiveness

Alan K. Campbell
Visiting Executive Professor
The Wharton School
University of Pennsylvania

James M. Cannon
Consultant
The Eisenhower Centennial
    Foundation

William D. Carey
Senior Consultant
Carnegie Corporation of New York

Harry L. Carrico
Chief Justice
Supreme Court of Virginia

Garrey E. Carruthers
Former Governor
State of New Mexico

Ashton B. Carter
Director
Center for Science and
    International Affairs
Harvard University

Jimmy Carter
Former President of the United
    States

Richard F. Celeste
Former Governor
State of Ohio

Lawton Chiles
Governor
State of Florida

Mary Clutter
Assistant Director, Biological,
    Behavioral & Social Sciences
National Science Foundation

Christopher Coburn
Director, Public Technology
    Programs
Battelle

William T. Coleman, Jr.
Senior Attorney
O'Melveny & Myers

Theodore Cooper
Chairman & Chief Executive
    Officer
The Upjohn Company

Douglas M. Costle
Former Administrator
U.S. Environmental Protection
    Agency

Eugene H. Cota-Robles
Special Assistant for Human
    Resources and Affirmative
    Action
National Science Foundation

Kenneth W. Dam
Max Pam Professor of American
    and Foreign Law
University of Chicago

Edward E. David
EED Corporation

John M. Deutch
Institute Professor
Massachusetts Institute of
     Technology

William Drayton
President
Ashoka: Innovators for the Public

Sidney D. Drell
Professor and Deputy Director
Stanford Linear Accelerator Center

Kathryn L. Edmundson
President
CBS Foundation

Thomas Ehrlich
President
Indiana University

Stuart E. Eizenstat
Partner
Powell, Goldstein, Frazer & Murphy

E. Donald Elliott
Professor of Law
Yale Law School

Daniel J. Evans
Chairman
Daniel J. Evans Associates

John R. Evans
Chairman of the Board
The Rockefeller Foundation

Kenneth R. Feinberg
Attorney
Kenneth R. Feinberg and Associates

Alexandra M. Field
Program Associate
Carnegie Commission on Science,
     Technology, and Government

Gerald R. Ford
Former President of the United States

John S. Foster, Jr.
TRW, Inc.

Robert W. Fri
President
Resources for the Future

Edward A. Frieman
Director
Scripps Institution of Oceanography

Robert A. Frosch
Vice President
General Motors Research
     Laboratories

Steven G. Gallagher
Senior Staff Associate
Carnegie Commission on Science,
     Technology, and Government

Stephen J. Gage
President
Cleveland Advanced Manufacturing
     Program

John H. Gibbons
Assistant to the President for Science
     and Technology and
Director, Office of Science and
     Technology Policy

William T. Golden
Chairman of the Board
American Museum of Natural
     History

Ralph E. Gomory
President
Alfred P. Sloan Foundation

General Andrew J. Goodpaster (Ret.)
Chairman
Atlantic Council of The United States

Christina E. Halvorson
Program Assistant
Carnegie Commission on Science,
     Technology, and Government

David A. Hamburg
President
Carnegie Corporation of New York

Edgar C. Harrell
Director, Operations and Programs
International Privatization Group
Price Waterhouse

Paul Harris, Jr.
Operations Manager
Carnegie Commission on Science,
     Technology, and Government

Philip Hemily
Office of International Affairs
National Academy of Sciences

Robert J. Hermann
Senior Vice President, Science and
     Technology
United Technologies Corporation

Rev. Theodore M. Hesburgh
President Emeritus
University of Notre Dame

A. Bryce Hoflund
Staff Assistant
Carnegie Commission on Science, Technology, and Government

Lilli Hornig
Senior Consultant, Higher Education Resources Services
Wellesley College

Alice Householder
Research Assistant
Carnegie Commission on Science, Technology, and Government

William G. Howard, Jr.
Senior Fellow
National Academy of Engineering

Shirley M. Hufstedler
Attorney
Hufstedler, Kaus & Ettinger

Admiral B. R. Inman
USN (Retired)

E. Pendleton James
Pendleton James & Associates

Rollin B. Johnson
John F. Kennedy School of Government
Harvard University

H. Graham Jones
Executive Director
New York State Science and Technology Foundation

Helene L. Kaplan
Attorney
Skadden, Arps, Slate, Meagher & Flom

Bruce W. Karrh
Vice President for Integrated Health Care
Du Pont Company

Robert W. Kastenmeier
Chairman
National Commission on Judicial Discipline and Removal

Robert Kates
University Professor Emeritus
Brown University

William M. Kaula
Professor of Geophysics
Department of Earth and Space Sciences
University of California

David Kearns
Under Secretary of Education
Department of Education

Kenneth H. Keller
The Phillip D. Reed Senior Fellow for Science & Technology
Council on Foreign Relations

Donald Kennedy
Bing Professor of Environmental Science, Institute for International Studies and President Emeritus
Stanford University

Alexander Keynan
Professor
The Hebrew University of Jerusalem

David A. Kirsch
Program Associate
Carnegie Commission on Science, Technology, and Government

Pamela S. Kulik
Staff Assistant
Carnegie Commission on Science, Technology, and Government

Joshua Lederberg
University Professor
Rockefeller University

Leon M. Lederman
Director Emeritus
Fermi National Accelerator Laboratory

John P. Lewis
Professor of Economics and International Affairs Emeritus
Woodrow Wilson Center
Princeton University

Dolores Locascio
Administrative Assistant
Carnegie Commission on Science, Technology, and Government

Stephen J. Lukasik
Vice President and Chief Scientist
TRW, Inc.

Gordon J. F. MacDonald
Director of Policy Studies
Institute on Global Conflict and
    Cooperation
University of California, San Diego

G. Calvin MacKenzie
Professor of Government
Colby College

Lydia Makhubu
Vice-Chancellor
University of Swaziland

Thomas F. Malone
Adjunct Professor
Department of Marine, Earth, and
    Atmospheric Sciences
North Carolina State University

Walter E. Massey
Director
National Science Foundation

Charles McC. Mathias, Jr.
Attorney
Jones, Day, Reavis & Pogue

Doris Manville
Administrative Assistant
Carnegie Commission on Science,
    Technology, and Government

Shirley M. McBay
President
Quality Education for Minorities
    (QEM) Network

Lawrence McCray
Executive Director
Committee on Science,
    Technology, and Public Policy
National Academy of Sciences

Michael McGeary
Study Director
National Research Council

Francis E. McGovern
Professor of Law
University of Alabama

Peter McPherson
Executive Vice President
Latin America and Canada Division
Bank of America

John P. McTague
Vice President for Technical Affairs
Ford Motor Company

Simone Mechaly
Staff Assistant
Carnegie Commission on Science,
    Technology, and Government

Richard A. Merrill
Professor of Law
University of Virginia

Richard A. Meserve
Partner
Covington & Burling

Howard Messner
Executive Vice President
American Consulting Engineers
    Council

Mary Ellen Mogee
President
Mogee Research and Analysis
    Associates

David Mosher
Nuclear Weapons Analyst
National Security Division
Congressional Budget Office

Frank E. Mosier
Vice Chairman, Advisory Board
BP America, Inc.

Rodney W. Nichols
Chief Executive Officer
New York Academy of Sciences

Janet L. Norwood
Senior Fellow
The Urban Institute

Philip A. Odeen
President & Chief Executive Officer
BDM International

Gilbert S. Omenn
Dean, School of Public Health and
    Community Medicine
University of Washington

David Packard
Chairman of the Board
Hewlett-Packard Company

Joseph G. Perpich
Vice President for Grants and
    Special Programs
Howard Hughes Medical Institute

William J. Perry
Chairman and Chief Executve Officer
Technology Strategies & Alliances

James Pfiffner
Consultant
National Research Council

Walter H. Plosila
President
Montgomery County High
    Technology Council, Inc.

Rutherford Poats
Consultant
The World Bank

Lewis F. Powell, Jr
Associate Justice (Ret.)
Supreme Court of the United States

Charles W. Powers
Managing Senior Partner
Resources for Responsible
    Management

Victor Rabinowitch
Vice President for Programs
MacArthur Foundation

Susan U. Raymond
Independent Consultant

Lauren B. Resnick
Director, Learning Research &
    Development Center
University of Pittsburgh

James B. Reston
Senior Columnist (Retired)
New York Times

Paul D. Rheingold
Partner
Rheingold & McGowen, P.C.

Alice M. Rivlin
Senior Fellow
Economics Department
Brookings Institution

David Z. Robinson
Executive Director
Carnegie Commission on Science,
    Technology, and Government

Maxine L. Rockoff
Senior Administrator
Carnegie Commission on Science,
    Technology, and Government

Paul Rogers
Partner
Hogan & Hartson

Maryann Roper
Science Consultant
The Carter Center of Emory
    University

Maurice Rosenberg
Professor of Law
Columbia University

Walter A. Rosenblith
Institute Professor
Massachusetts Institute of Technology

Patricia L. Rosenfield
Program Chair
Strengthening Human Resources in
    Developing Countries
Carnegie Corporation of New York

Elspeth Rostow
Stiles Professor in American Studies
    and Professor of Government
LBJ School of Public Affairs
University of Texas

Oscar M. Ruebhausen
Retired Presiding Partner
Debevoise & Plimpton

Avery Russell
Director of Publications and
    Program Officer
Carnegie Corporation of New York

F. James Rutherford
Chief Education Officer and
    Director, Project 2061
Office of Science & Technology
    Education
American Association for the
    Advancement of Science

Pamela Ann Rymer
U.S. Circuit Judge
U.S. Court of Appeals for
    the Ninth Circuit

Francisco Sagasti
Principal Investigator
Grupo de Analisis Para el Desarrolo
    (Peru)

Jonas Salk
Founding Director
Salk Institute for Biological Studies

John Sawyer
Retired President
The Mellon Foundation

Mark Schaefer
Senior Staff Associate and
    Director, Washington Office
Carnegie Commission on Science,
    Technology, and Government

Roland W. Schmitt
President
Rensselaer Polytechnic Institute

Alan Schriesheim
Director
Argonne National Laboratory

Charles Schultze
Senior Fellow of Economics
Brookings Institution

Robert L. Seamans, Jr.
Senior Lecturer
Department of Aeronautics and
    Astronautics
Massachusetts Institute of
    Technology

Donna Shalala
Chancellor
University of Wisconsin

Irving S. Shapiro
Retired Chairman and Chief
    Executive Officer
DuPont Company

Willis H. Shapley
Former Senior Staff Member
Bureau of the Budget

George P. Shultz, Jr.
Former Secretary of State
Stanford University

Maxine F. Singer
President
Carnegie Institution of Washington

Linda S. Dix Skidmore
Study Director
Committee on Science and
    Engineering
National Academy of Sciences

Eugene Skolnikoff
Professor of Political Science
Massachusetts Institute of
    Technology

Lori D. Skopp
Program Associate
Carnegie Commission on Science,
    Technology, and Government

William K. Slate, II
President
Justice Research Institute

Bruce L. R. Smith
Senior Staff
Center for Public Policy Education
Brookings Institution

Robert M. Solow
Institute Professor
Department of Economics
Massachusetts Institute of
    Technology

Elmer B. Staats
Chairman of the Board
Harry S. Truman Scholarship
    Foundation

H. Guyford Stever
Former Director
National Science Foundation

Vivien Stewart
Program Chair
Education and Healthy
    Development of Children and
    Youth
Carnegie Corporation of New York

Marcia Sward
Executive Director
Mathematical Association of
    America

John Temple Swing
Executive Vice President
Council on Foreign Relations

John F. Trattner
Vice President
Council for Excellence in
    Government

Dick Thornburgh
Undersecretary General
Department of Administration and
    Management
United Nations

David G. Victor
Political Science Department
Massachusetts Institute of
    Technology

Patricia M. Wald
U.S. Circuit Judge
U.S. Court of Appeals for the
    District of Columbia Circuit

APPENDIX E
BIOGRAPHIES OF AUTHORS

NORMAN R. AUGUSTINE is Chairman and Chief Executive Officer of the Martin Marietta Corporation. He served as Undersecretary of the Army from 1975 to 1977 and as Assistant Secretary from 1973 to 1975. He chaired the Defense Science Board from 1966 to 1970 and was Assistant Director of Defense Research and Engineering from 1965 to 1970. Mr. Augustine was a member of the U.S. Air Force Science Advisory Board and of the Chief of Naval Operations Executive Panel.

JOHN BRADEMAS is president emeritus of New York University, which he joined in 1981. For twenty-two years (1959–1981) Dr. Brademas served as United States Representative in Congress from Indiana, the last four as House Majority Whip. Dr. Brademas is chairman, by appointment of Governor Mario Cuomo, of the New York State Council on Fiscal and Economic Priorities.

LEWIS M. BRANSCOMB is the Albert Pratt Public Service Professor at the John F. Kennedy School of Government of Harvard University. A research physicist, Dr. Branscomb was appointed director of the National Bureau of Standards by the President in 1969. He joined the Bureau in 1951, served as chief of the NBS Atomic Physics Division, and was co-founder and chairman of the Joint Intitute for Laboratory Astrophysics at the University of Colorado before his appointment as director of NBS. In 1979, Dr. Branscomb was appointed by President Carter to the National Science Board, and in 1980 he was elected chairman, serving until May 1984. Dr. Branscomb joined International Business Machines as vice president and chief scientist in 1972. In 1983 he was named a member of the Corporate Management Board and in 1985 a director of the IBM World Trade Europe/Middle East/Africa Corporation.

WILLIAM D. CAREY was CEO of the American Association for the Advancement of Science from 1975 to 1987. He is currently a senior consultant to Carnegie Corporation of New York. Before joining Carnegie, he served as vice president of Arthur D. Little, Inc., following a long career as Assistant Director in the Bureau of the Budget, Executive Office of the President.

FORMER PRESIDENT JIMMY CARTER is the founder of the Atlanta-based Carter Center, a nonprofit organization that works to resolve conflict, promote democracy, preserve human rights, improve health, and fight hunger around the world. Through nonpartisan study and outreach programs, the Center has addressed the prospects for peace in the Middle East, monitored elections in Latin America, mediated conflicts in the Horn of Africa, and made significant progress in improving the health of people in developing countries. Before his election as President of the United States in 1976, Mr. Carter served as Governor of Georgia and worked as a farmer and engineer.

RICHARD F. CELESTE was a two-term Governor of Ohio from 1983 to 1991. During his tenure he led an aggressive program to promote international trade and investment, with trade offices worldwide. At present, Celeste operates Celeste & Sabety Ltd., a company that specializes in providing linkages to world markets. Celeste has been actively involved in the fields of international technology and the role of governments in science, research, and development. As Governor, he chaired the National Governors Association Committee on Science and Technology. He is a member of the Advisory Board at Oak Ridge National Laboratories. From 1979 to 1981, Celeste directed the U.S. Peace Corps, which had programs in 53 countries. He served in the Foreign Service under Ambassador Chester Bowles in India from 1963 to 1967.

DOUGLAS M. COSTLE is former Dean of Vermont Law School. He is currently Distinguished Senior Fellow at the Institute for Sustainable Communities, of which he was also a co-founder. Dean Costle was a trial attorney in the Civil Rights Division of the U.S. Department of Justice and served as an attorney for the U.S. Department of Commerce, Economic Development Administration. Costle also served as Commissioner of the Connecticut Department of Environmental Protection, Assistant Director of the U.S. Congressional Budget Office, and Administrator of the U.S. Environmental Protection Agency.

ROBERT W. FRI is president of Resources for the Future, an independent nonprofit organization that conducts research and policy analysis on issues affecting natural resources and environmental quality. He received a BA with Honors in Physics from Rice University and an MBA from Harvard. From 1971 to 1975 he served as first deputy administrator and then as acting administrator of the Environmental Protection Agency. From 1975 to 1977 he served as first deputy administrator and then as acting administrator of the Energy and Research and Development Administration. Before joining Resources for the Future he was a member of the management consulting firm McKinsey and Company and was president of the Energy Transition Corporation, which engaged in new energy product development. He is a trustee of the Environmental and Energy Study Institute, Science Service, Inc., and the Atlantic Council of the U.S. and a member of the Advisory Council of the Electric Power Research Institute, Phi Beta Kappa, and Sigma Xi.

WILLIAM T. GOLDEN is chairman of the American Museum of Natural History and an officer and trustee of several scientific and educational organizations, including the New York Academy of Sciences (life governor) and the American Association for the Advancement of Science (treasurer). Mr. Golden served as an officer in the U.S. Navy on active duty throughout World War II, and has served in the Atomic Energy Commission, the Department of State, and the Executive Office of the President. As Special Consultant to President Truman (1950–1951) to review the organization of the Government's scientific activities incident to the Korean War, Mr. Golden designed the first Presidential Science Advisory apparatus, recommending creation of a Science Advisor to the President and of the President's Science Advisory Committee (PSAC).

DAVID A. HAMBURG has been President of Carnegie Corporation of New York since 1983. A medical doctor by training, Dr. Hamburg was President of the Institute of Medicine from 1975 to 1980. He was Director of the Division of Health Policy Research and Education and John D. MacArthur Professor of Health Policy at Harvard University from 1980 to 1982. He served as President, then Chairman of the Board of the American Association for the Advancement of Science from 1984 to 1986. Dr. Hamburg is a trustee and vice chairman of the board of Stanford University. In science policy, he has served as chairman of several national groups, including the Science Policy Committee of the Institute of Medicine and both the intramural and extramural Scientific Advisory Boards of the National Institute of Mental Health.

ADMIRAL B. R. INMAN (Ret.), currently a private investor, was Chairman, President, and Chief Executive Officer of Westmark Systems, Inc. from 1986 to 1989 and Chairman, President, and Chief Executive Officer of Microelectronics and Computer Technology Corporation from 1983 to 1986. Admiral Inman served as Deputy Director of Central Intelligence from 1981 to 1982, Director of the National Security Agency from 1977 to 1981, Vice Director of the Defense Intelligence Agency from 1976 to 1977, and Director of Naval Intelligence from 1974 to 1976. He served as Vice Chairman of the President's Foreign Intelligence Advisory Board from July 1990 to January 1993.

HELENE L. KAPLAN is Of Counsel to Skadden, Arps, Slate, Meagher & Flom, concentrating in not-for-profit and fiduciary law. Mrs. Kaplan has served in the not-for-profit sector as counsel or trustee of many scientific, arts, charitable, and educational institutions and foundations. She chairs the Board of Trustees of Barnard College and serves as treasurer of the Association of the Bar of the City of New York. Former chairman of the Board of Trustees of Carnegie Corporation of New York, Mrs. Kaplan currently serves as a trustee of that foundation. From 1985 to 1987, she was a member of the U.S. Secretary of State's Advisory Committee on South Africa; and from 1986 to 1990, she served as a member of the New York State Governor's Task Force on Life and the Law, concerned with the legal and ethical implications of advances in medical technology. Mrs. Kaplan is a director of several corporate boards. She is member of the American Academy of Arts and Sciences, the American Philosophical Society, and the Council on Foreign Relations.

JOSHUA LEDERBERG, a research geneticist, is University Professor and President emeritus of The Rockefeller University. Dr. Lederberg pioneered in the field of bacterial genetics with the discovery of genetic recombination in bacteria. In 1958, at the age of 33, Dr. Lederberg received the Nobel Prize in Physiology or Medicine for this work and subsequent research on bacterial genetics. A member of the National Academy of Sciences since 1957 and a charter member of its Institute of Medicine, Dr. Lederberg has been active on many government advisory committees and boards, such as NIH study sections and the National Advisory Mental Health Council, and has served as chairman of the President's Cancer Panel.

THOMAS MALONE is a former foreign secretary of the National Academy of Sciences. The editor of the Compendium of Meteorology, Dr. Malone received his Ph.D. from MIT. From 1956 to 1970 Dr. Malone was with the Traveler's Insurance Company, where he became a senior vice president. Dr. Malone was the founding secretary general of the Scientific Committee on Problems of the Environment (SCOPE) of the International Council of Scientific Unions (ICSU) and was also vice president of ICSU. Dr. Malone is currently based at the Department of Marine, Earth, and Atmospheric Sciences of North Carolina State University and serves as director of the Sigma Xi Scholars Center.

RODNEY W. NICHOLS is Chief Executive Officer of The New York Academy of Sciences. He served as vice president and executive vice president of The Rockefeller University from 1970 to 1990, following R&D assignments in industry and the Office of the Secretary of Defense. One of the leaders of the U.S. delegation to the 1979 UN Conference on Science and Technology for Development, he has served as a consultant on international S&T policy. Mr. Nichols was Scholar-in-Residence at Carnegie Corporation of New York from 1990 to 1992.

WILLIAM J. PERRY was Chairman of Technology Strategies & Alliances, Inc., and a professor in the School of Engineering and Co-Director of the Center for International Security and Arms Control at Stanford University, until his recent designation as Deputy Secretary of Defense. He was Undersecretary of Defense for Research and Engineering from 1977 to 1981 and President of ESL, Inc. from 1964 to 1977. He is a member of the National Academy of Engineering and a member of the National Academy of Sciences' Committee on International Security and Arms Control. Dr. Perry has served on the Defense Science Board, the President's Foreign Intelligence Advisory Board, and the Aspen Strategy Group of the Aspen Institute for Humanistic Studies.

H. GUYFORD STEVER was Director of the National Science Foundation from 1972 to 1976; during this time he also served as Science Advisor to Presidents Nixon and Ford. He was Director of the White House Office of Science and Technology Policy from 1976 to 1977. Before joining NSF, he was Professor of Aeronautics and Astronautics at MIT from 1945 to 1965 and was President of Carnegie–Mellon University from 1965 to 1972. He was also Chief Scientist of the Air Force in 1955 and 1956. Dr. Stever is a member of the National Academy of Sciences, the National Academy of Engineering, and the American Academy of Arts and Sciences; a fellow of the American Physical Society, the American Institute of Aeronautics and Astronautics, the Royal Astronautical Society, and the Royal Society of Arts; a foreign associate of the Japan Academy of Engineering, and a foreign member of Britain's Fellowship of Engineering. Dr. Stever received the National Medal of Science in 1991.

PHOTOGRAPH CREDITS

Page 12, The White House
Leo de Wys/Svat Macha

Page 16, The Capitol
Leo de Wys/Radie Nedlin

Page 20, Court House, Augusta, Georgia
Leo de Wys/Bill Grimes

Page 24, Old Glory
Uniphoto/Les Moore

Page 28, Inside the State Department
U.S. Department of State

Page 32, Hooghly River and Calcutta
Christopher Warren

Page 36, The Earth from space
Leo de Wys

Page 40, The Brandenburg Gate, Berlin,
    November 1989
AP/Wide World Photos

Page 44, A robot hand
Uniphoto/David Mallory Jones

Page 48, High school graduation
Uniphoto/Melanie Carr

Page 52, Weather balloon
Uniphoto/Daemmerich

Page 56, The bald eagle
Leo de Wys

Page 60, The Global Forum
Women's Environment and Development
    Organization

Page 64, Robert Oppenheimer
AP/Wide World Photos

Page 68, Young scientists, Timberlane Junior
    School, Pennington, New Jersey
Donna Aster